Crowdfunded

The Proven Path To Bring Your Product Idea To Life

Mark Pecota

CEO OF LAUNCHBOOM

DOWNLOAD THE AUDIOBOOK FREE

My book is only valuable once you start to read it. It's even more valuable if you finish it.

That's why I'm giving you the audiobook version too, and it's 100 percent FREE.

You can listen to it while doing chores, or during your commute. I even narrated the book myself!

SCAN OR GO TO CROWDFUNDEDBOOK.COM/AUDIO

VIDEO SUMMARY

Would you like a video summary of this book that'll help you start making progress on your launch quickly?

Check out my video training and overview of the process.

In the training, I cover three things:

| Why crowdfunding is the most effective way to launch a product | How to build a prelaunch email list of people who are thirty times more likely to buy | How to launch and get funded on the very first day of your campaign |

SCAN OR GO TO CROWDFUNDEDBOOK.COM/SUMMARY

Want Our Help At LaunchBoom?

Do you want some help implementing the content in this book?

We're here. At LaunchBoom, our goal is to help you launch a successful product, and save you hundreds of hours and thousands of dollars in the process.

If you want to go faster and further with your launch and you're serious about getting help, book a call with my team. We'll put together a launch plan and show you how we can work together.

SCAN OR GO TO CROWDFUNDEDBOOK.COM/CALL

Printed in the United States of America.

ISBN: 9798397169882

Thank you to Ricardo Melo for your beautiful cover and graphic design, Jill Bailin for your detailed editing, and Gilbert Rafanan for your amazing book layout design.

DEDICATION

I'd like to dedicate this book to the following people:

My Parents

As a child, I thought I'd be a rockstar. During my college years, I thought I'd be an electronic music producer. Now, I'm launching products. Whatever I chose to focus on in my life, my parents were always there to support me. The values they taught me and the love they gave me shaped me into who I am. I'll always be grateful.

My Partners

There is no way I could have built LaunchBoom (or written this book) without the support of my business partners Will Ford, Mike Revie, and Victor Shiu. Thank you for sticking with me through thick and thin.

My Team

The LaunchBoom team (both current and past) are the most talented, driven, and supportive people I have ever met. Thank you so much for the work you put in every day to change people's lives through launches.

Table of Contents

INTRODUCTION

CHAPTER 1

Launches Change Lives

Hey, I'm Mark Pecota, the CEO and co-founder of LaunchBoom. Even though this is probably our first "meeting," I can assure you that I'm excited for whatever you're launching. You see, I have a thing for helping creators launch their products. It still feels like Christmas morning every time I wake up at the crack of dawn to watch our team press the "launch" button — and watch while we raise tens of thousands of dollars in a matter of minutes.

Raising a lot of money in a short amount of time is great, but it's not really *why* I do this. The real gift is literally watching our clients' lives change. It might sound a little cheesy, but it's true.

Let's take Bubba from Give'r, for example. In 2016, Bubba was working as a baggage handler at Jackson Hole Airport while we were launching his first product, the 4-Season Gloves. After raising $270,942 at the beginning of that year, we had not only launched the Give'r brand, but we had launched a new trajectory for Bubba's life. Flash forward to today — he's built Give'r into a powerhouse and we continue to work with him. Our latest launch with Bubba did $198K within sixteen hours and ended up raising over a million dollars.

And look at Ridge from Rising Empire Studios. He came to us with a vision of creating different franchises under the Rising Empire Studios umbrella. Just the way that Marvel owns the Spider-Man, X-Men, and Iron Man franchises, Ridge wanted to do something similar. The problem was that he didn't know the best marketing strategy. So we helped him with that. We launched his Alpha Clash graphic novel on Kickstarter in June of 2022 and raised $59,150. Five months later, the second campaign for the Alpha Clash Trading Card Game was launched, and raised $422,809 on Kickstarter. Now, Ridge is gearing up to expand his first franchise with more products launching in 2023, all possible because of Kickstarter.

And this is my favorite story: In 2013, Kevin Liang from Aqua Design Innovations came to us with his product, the EcoQube. As it was our first crowdfunding launch ever, we had much to learn, but we still raised $79,026. Since then, we launched six more products with Kevin, raised millions of dollars, and ultimately Kevin went on to sell his very successful business.

How I Discovered Crowdfunding

It was the beginning of 2013. I had just finished my studies at sunny San Diego State University. Walking back to my car after my last class, I felt free, wide-eyed, as if the world was entirely available to me. Leaving the chains of student-hood behind, I felt liberated. I felt a sense of adventure awaiting me in the unknown. I was pretty sure I knew the next step I wanted to take, but I couldn't have had a clear idea of what I would be getting myself into.

You see, in my last semester, I'd gone through an intensive digital marketing internship, and while completing it left me feeling a bit relieved, more importantly, I felt incredibly excited to start my own venture.

The digital marketing skills I'd learned were valuable, but more valuable still were Mike and Tom, two guys I'd met in my internship. In the final weeks we decided that we should give a shot to starting our own digital marketing agency. Our only rule was that we would have to close a deal before the internship – and the comfort of our college careers – was over.

Somehow, we did close a $5,000 deal with a law firm. I remember the feeling of driving away from that meeting as if it were yesterday. A flood of emotions overwhelmed me – excitement, joy, confidence, and pride, all sprinkled with a bit of disbelief that we were actually doing this. I still have that first signed contract by my desk. It serves as a small reminder of where we came from.

The name of our company then was Label Creative. Part of me would love to tell you how cutting-edge our company was, but to be frank, there wasn't anything innovative or particularly unique about what we started. We were a marketing agency, just like the thousands of other marketing agencies providing digital marketing, video production, web design, and branding services.

With that said, the major difference between us and everyone else was our team. I had never worked around a group of individuals more curious and hungry to grow — both personally and professionally. Those values guided us to say "yes" to all types of projects outside of our core expertise.

Even though we were exposed to many different types of projects and companies, that wasn't the best way to scale a business. But I don't regret anything, because it led us to Kevin.

Our first crowdfunding experience was with Kevin Liang (as I mentioned earlier). He came to us and asked for support launching his product EcoQube on Kickstarter. We'd heard of Kickstarter before, but had no experience using the platform. It sounded like a great opportunity, so we took the job. Flash forward a couple of months – and we had raised $79,026 for EcoQube.

After seeing the success of the first campaign, we were quick to launch a new product. This time we launched on Indiegogo for our client 1Hour Break, and raised $105,343. Shortly after that, Kevin came back with a new product called EcoQube C, and we raised $375,058 on Kickstarter.

We were astounded by the massive success of our third campaign. Launching products through crowdfunding was powerful... and more people needed to know about it!

Helping Others Tap into the Power of Crowdfunding

Very soon after our second Kickstarter launch with Kevin, I knew we had to change our focus. It was fun saying "yes" to all types of projects at Label Creative, but every "yes" that wasn't a crowdfunding launch began to seem like a waste of time, and even worse, a wasted opportunity. Crowdfunding was (and still is) a very new industry, and I wanted to show more product creators what was possible.

Now all we needed was a name.

Driving up to north county San Diego, I remember being stuck in traffic when I got a call from Will Ford, one of my business partners.

"What's up, Will?" I said.

"LaunchBoom!" Will answered.

"What?" I wasn't sure I heard him right.

"LaunchBoom," he said again. "*That's* what we're calling this thing. I just bought the domain!"

It was perfect. So, with the perfect name, team, and vision for what we were going to create, we shut down Label Creative and rebranded as LaunchBoom at the end of 2015. We could start to spread the good news of crowdfunding to entrepreneurs worldwide.

Since we began LaunchBoom, we've built a team consisting of more than twenty experts, we've worked with thousands of entrepreneurs from more than forty countries, and we've raised over $100 million (and believe me when I tell you, we haven't stopped!). Kickstarter and Indiegogo, the top crowdfunding platforms, have both recognized LaunchBoom as "certified experts."

As you can probably guess, I have learned *a lot* about what to do and what not to do when it comes to launching products. It's been quite the journey, with some very big wins and a few setbacks, of course, but each obstacle taught us new lessons that I'm excited to share with you.

Updates Since the First Edition of This Book

I published the first edition of *Crowdfunded* in April of 2020, and it's been downloaded and purchased by tens of thousands of people since then. I've heard from hundreds of readers who were able to bring their product ideas to life just because they read this book. The reception has been incredible.

Since publishing the first edition, we've helped more than 500 Launch-Boom clients launch their products, drive tens of millions of dollars in revenue, and create real, profitable businesses.

In that same time, we launched the *Crowdfunded Summit*, which is now the biggest summit on crowdfunding in the world. We've also overhauled our system at least five times, and we've built software and tech used by thousands of people all over the world.

We've also launched highly successful campaigns in many different categories. Most of the previous edition of this book concerned design and technology products. But since then, we've launched boutique hotels, graphic novels, and tabletop games, which are just a few of the areas we're branching out in.

Needless to say, every part of our launch system has gotten significantly better. So I decided to update *Crowdfunded* and include our new knowledge in this second edition. These up-to-date strategies, frameworks, and templates will save you hundreds of hours and thousands of dollars as you proceed.

An Overview of What You'll Learn

First, I'll introduce you to the seven key milestones you need to achieve to go from product idea to successful crowdfunding launch. I call this the "Product Idea to *Crowdfunded*" framework. They are:

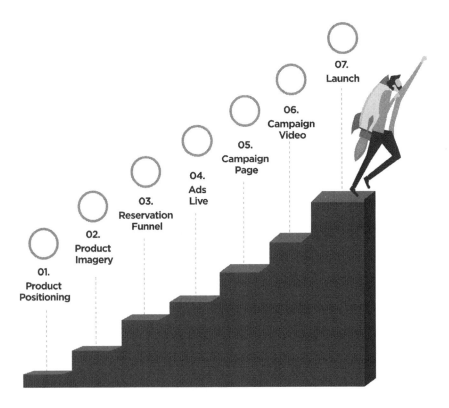

After you learn about the Product Idea to *Crowdfunded* framework, I'll show you the next steps on your *Crowdfunded* Creator journey.

I'll teach you how to boost your campaign once you've had a successful launch. I'll teach you how to transition smoothly to the post-campaign (and raise more money through pledge managers). I'll even teach you how to leverage your launch to start scaling through e-commerce.

By the end of this book, you'll understand every key milestone necessary to turn your product idea into a real e-commerce business.

What to Expect from This Book

This book is a practical, no-nonsense guide based on what's actually worked for me and for thousands of other entrepreneurs like you.

My goal here is to "drop the mic." I want this to not only be the *best* book you'll read on the topic, but the *only* book you'll need to read and keep by your side to launch a successful campaign.

Once you finish the book, I want you to feel 100 percent clear on the path forward. I want you to implement what you learn and save yourself hundreds of hours and thousands of dollars in the process. I want you to feel confident that now is the time to get off the sidelines and *finally* bring your product idea to life.

And anytime someone is thinking of launching a product, my hope is that you'll want to tell them, "You *have* to read *Crowdfunded*."

If you want to go even faster and further with your launch, I believe that *Crowdfunded* is the first step in us working together. When you're ready, book a call with my team to see if we're a good fit, and we'll map out a launch plan to get started.

This book will be your field guide as you navigate the unknown path of launching your product. Read it through and keep it close. By the end of it, you'll feel clear and confident. Clear on the path you must take to succeed. Confident that you *will* bring your idea to life.

Ready? Let's start!

CHAPTER

The Power of Crowdfunding

At the end of 2022, Kickstarter passed a huge milestone: **$7 billion raised on their platform**. If you add Indiegogo's stats, the number would be over $10 billion. That's a lot of revenue for new product launches.

It's been ten years since we launched our first crowdfunding campaign with the EcoQube. That's a long time to dedicate yourself to anything. So why am I still here? The answer is simple.

Because crowdfunding is *still* so powerful.

For product creators whose products are unique, I haven't yet seen a better way to launch. For one thing, nothing decreases risk more than leveraging crowdfunding. And as entrepreneurs, everything we do is risky…so risk mitigation is key.

There are five core concepts that make crowdfunding so effective. These ideas explain why I'm still dedicated to helping product creators use crowdfunding to bring their ideas to life. And why I think you should, too.

Concept #1: Generate revenue without inventory

Traditional product launches are incredibly risky. Product creators invest a great deal of time and money in developing their product.

They go through a manufacturing run so they have inventory. Then they spend a massive amount of money on their marketing strategy. When they go to launch, they pray that the sales come in. If not, they'll be sitting on thousands of units (and many, many, many dollars) of inventory.

Crowdfunding offers product creators a different, less risky path. All the product creator needs is a prototype. Seriously, that's it.

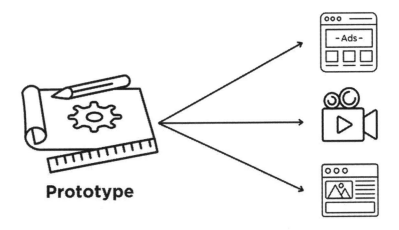

Prototype

With that prototype, an entire crowdfunding campaign can be built. Since backers are pre-ordering your product, you'll receive all the money before you go to manufacture.

Ideally, you'll be able to place a larger-volume order with your manufacturer because of the success you'll have through crowdfunding. And larger-volume orders usually decrease the cost per unit and increase your margin. Because companies can leverage economies of scale by capitalizing on presale orders and reducing their financial risk, this is a beautiful model.

Concept #2: Validate demand for your new product

In the traditional product launch model, product creators sink huge amounts of money into product design and manufacturing before they've sold anything. Once they have inventory, they start to invest heavily in marketing.

With crowdfunding, we flip the model.

You'll spend more money on marketing before you create the product. You'll be able to validate demand for your product and answer other key business questions *before* you invest in inventory. The questions you'll have to answer are these:

- Can I acquire a customer profitably?
- What product positioning is most effective?
- Which audiences respond best to my product?

Answering those questions will allow you to proceed into the manufacturing phase confidently. More importantly, since you invested time and money into marketing during your presale, you can hit the ground running when you transition to e-commerce.

Concept #3: Tap into a community of early adopters

On average, Kickstarter and Indiegogo combined receive tens of millions of unique visitors per month. That's an extremely large group of potential customers to tap into.

But more than just being an extremely large group, this is a *vibrant* community that is constantly looking for new ideas to back and get behind. That translates to a group of people who are ready to spend money on your product and become "super fans" for your brand.

At LaunchBoom, we like to characterize backers on Kickstarter and Indiegogo as people who "want cool stuff, at a discount, before anyone else."

Let's take this description and apply it to the famous "product adoption curve." This curve represents the different groups of people who adopt new technology, ideas, or products, with everyone after "early adopters" considered as the mass market.

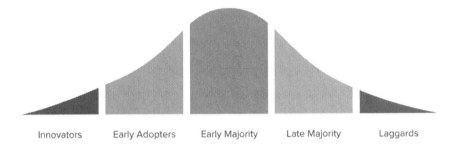

| Innovators | Early Adopters | Early Majority | Late Majority | Laggards |

The "innovators" and "early adopters" are people who back crowdfunding projects. These are the people willing to take more risk with the products they buy. That's because they are largely motivated to be the *first* to know about something. We all have those friends who knew about that new popular thing "before it was popular." Well, crowdfunding backers are like that. They're on top of what's new.

Each platform allows their community to browse live campaigns. Projects are ranked on a number of factors, but ranking is largely driven by project popularity. Meaning, if you are able to drive a lot of sales early on, you are much more likely to have higher placement in the rankings and, ultimately, more traffic to your campaign.

Tapping into this community allows your marketing dollars to go much further because you don't have to pay anything for the additional traffic (besides the 5 percent platform fee on funds raised). Across all our campaigns, we find that at least 20 percent of funds raised comes from organic traffic on the crowdfunding platform. That's a huge lift that definitely makes up for the 5 percent fee you'll be paying Kickstarter or Indiegogo.

Concept #4: Improve your product with feedback

Crowdfunding campaigns are a low-risk way to get feedback from your customers before you make your product.

We've seen backers provide feedback that led to product break-throughs. We've seen the price of a product change based on customer comments. We've seen creators save thousands of dollars on additional product variants (like colors or sizes) simply by asking their community which alternatives they wanted.

All of the information you gather during your campaign will lay the foundation for the future success of your product and your company.

At the end of the day, the beauty of crowdfunding is your community of backers. They know your product is improving and are willing to invest their ideas, money, and social reach to ensure its success. These early customers can be your most loyal fans and give you great feedback to make your product and business better. They will also post your first reviews when you move to e-commerce, giving you immediate credibility when you start to scale.

Concept #5: Position yourself for bigger deals

Once you deliver a successful crowdfunding campaign, you've proven that there's a demand for your product. I've seen this significantly benefit entrepreneurs and help them close bigger deals for their business.

They've connected with distributors and retailers, received licensing opportunities, or raised capital through debt or equity. We've even seen many product creators get massive exposure on *Shark Tank*!

You can leverage your success for future press as well. Crowdfunding is social by nature. Your success will be disseminated across social media by your newfound community and will always live on the crowdfunding platform. We've helped our clients use this credibility to continue building their brand through e-commerce.

Now You Understand The Why

Crowdfunding offers a new, better approach for product creators. It requires less risk than traditional product launches. It's the reason I've dedicated myself to this over the past ten years (although with each new thing I learn, sometimes it can still feel like I'm just getting started).

Next, let's dive into the mindset needed to take advantage of the power of crowdfunding.

CHAPTER

The Crowdfunded Creator Mindset

Now that you understand why crowdfunding is the best way to launch your product, you're one step closer to becoming a *Crowdfunded* Creator.

To become successful here, though, you will need to adopt the *Crowdfunded* Creator mindset. That requires you to identify some of your limiting beliefs.

This isn't "woo-woo" stuff I'm talking about. The truth is that the biggest thing in the way of success is *internal* – the obstacles lie within us, in some of our beliefs…

More specifically, the *limiting beliefs* we hold.

It's a good idea to address those limiting beliefs now, before you get started.

Limiting Belief #1: I don't have time to launch my product

This is the one I hear the most:

"But Mark, you don't get it. I don't have the time to launch my product. I'm so busy!"

The truth is that no one *has* the time for anything these days – they *make* the time. I've worked with creators who have full-time jobs and a family with young kids, who still manage to pull off a launch without killing themselves.

The secret is in (1) committing to making your launch happen, (2) creating a detailed plan, which this book gives you, and (3) scheduling time every day to work on your launch.

Launching a product isn't easy or fast, but it takes a lot less time than most people think.

Limiting Belief #2: The timing isn't right...yet

Does that sound familiar?

"I'll get to [insert thing you want to accomplish here] once I complete [insert excuse here]. It's just not the right time...yet!"

In almost every case, saying "it's not the right time" is simply a way to procrastinate. The truth is, the "right" time doesn't exist. We tell ourselves that as a way to put off doing that thing we need or want to do.

I get it: Starting up is always the hardest part. At the beginning it can seem impossible. But once you gain some momentum, it's hard to stop.

Limiting Belief #3: I'm not a marketer (I'm bad at it, or I hate it)

Most product creators love making their product, but hate marketing it (or they think they're bad at it). That's a problem.

You don't have to love marketing, but you do have to learn it. You may be thinking, "Well, I'm just going to outsource the marketing, so, no, I don't have to learn it."

Wrong.

Learning sales and marketing is key for success in any business. That doesn't mean you have to be an expert, but you do have to understand the fundamentals. Even if you hire someone down the road, understanding the fundamentals will help you choose a better person or company to work with.

Here's another way of thinking about it…

If you truly believe that people's lives will be better after using your product, it's your responsibility to do everything in your power to get them to buy and use your product. This includes getting over your fear or disdain of marketing.

Limiting Belief #4: I don't have a team

It can be daunting to look at everything that needs to be done and think it's impossible to do it – or even just start doing it – by yourself.

But that's not a valid worry.

Most people with whom I work on their product launches start out solo. Along the way, they were able to meet the right people, depending on what they needed at the time. They were never stuck, because the right resource was always out there. And the right resource will always be out there for you too.

We have a whole community here at LaunchBoom that you can be a part of, now that you own this book. Think of the *LaunchBoom Community* as your team. You don't have to do it alone.

Scan the QR code or go to crowdfundedbook.com/community to access the *LaunchBoom Community*.

Limiting Belief #5: I don't have enough money to launch on my own

I'm not going to tell you that bringing a product to life is cheap. But with the tools and resources available to product creators today (like this book), it's much more affordable than most people realize. Plus, there are many ways to dramatically reduce your risk in the prelaunch, launch, and post-launch phases. We'll get to that soon.

More important than saving up tens of thousands of dollars is *getting started*, and trying to validate whether or not your idea has demand.

Crowdfunding reduces your risk, since you can launch without inventory. Once you've proven demand, you can take the money you raise from Kickstarter and manufacture your product.

Limiting Belief #6: The launch might fail

Actually, the fact is that most crowdfunding launches fail. So fear of failure is perfectly understandable. But at the end of the day, failure is rarely as bad as we fear, and it shouldn't be the reason to stop yourself from launching.

What would you rather: (a) launch and fail…or (b) never launch and regret?

Regret is a deeper pain than failure, because at least with failure, you tried.

Limiting Belief #7: Who am I to launch a product? The impostor syndrome rears its head

Oh, the classic impostor syndrome. I remember being twenty-five years old and having people twice my age hire me to launch their products.

"Who am I to launch this product? I'm just a kid," I said to myself.

But as I've gotten older, it's occurred to me that most people don't always know what they're doing… *making me feel both more secure and more terrified at the same time.* People can know plenty of things sometimes, but the rest of the time, most people are just figuring it out as they go along, and there is nothing wrong with that.

Turn Limiting Beliefs into Empowering Beliefs

The first step in turning your limiting beliefs into empowering beliefs is to be aware of them. The next step is to understand why they exist. Hopefully, now, you're aware of your beliefs, and you understand why you have them (and why you shouldn't).

It's time for the last step: Turn the old limiting beliefs into empowering beliefs.

"It's not the right time…yet" turns into "I'm going to take the first step, now."

"I hate marketing" turns into "I love my customers and marketing connects me to them."

"What if my launch fails?" turns into "I'd rather launch and fail than never launch and regret."

Again, this mindset stuff may turn some of you off, but I guarantee it's important, especially at the beginning. Take the time to understand your own limiting beliefs and turn them into empowering beliefs. Doing so will allow you to adopt the *Crowdfunded* Creator mindset and set yourself up for launch success.

Let's start building your campaign

At this point, you understand *why* crowdfunding is such a powerful strategy for launching your product. It offers a new, better approach for entrepreneurs, which requires less risk and capital than traditional product launches. You also understand *why* your own limiting beliefs can be your biggest obstacle.

Now let's talk about the *how*. The rest of this book will be broken down into sections that go over each phase of the LaunchBoom system.

- **Part 1: Understanding the LaunchBoom System.** Before you get into the nitty-gritty of details, it's important to have a ten thousand–foot high aerial view of how it will work.
- **Part 2: Creating Your Reservation Funnel.** Position your product and make use of key marketing techniques to build LaunchBoom's reservation funnel, and set yourself up for success.
- **Part 3: Building Your Prelaunch Email List.** How to build a prelaunch email list that's thirty times more likely to buy your product.
- **Part 4: Getting Ready to Launch.** How to create your campaign video, campaign page, and build up hype for your launch.
- **Part 5: Launching a Successful Campaign.** How to have a "LaunchBoom" and hit your funding goal on the first day.
- **Part 6: Post-Campaign Tactics.** How to build on the momentum of your campaign and continue to pre-sell and upsell more product.

- **Part 7: Building a Long-Term Brand.** How to transition to e-commerce and scale your business.

Now, in the words of my friend and client, Bubba, from Give'r… buckle up! It's time to dive into the LaunchBoom System.

PART 1:
UNDERSTANDING THE LAUNCHBOOM SYSTEM

CHAPTER 4

The System

It's important for you to have a high-level understanding of the LaunchBoom System before we get into the nitty-gritty details. Once you can see the big picture, you'll be able to understand how everything connects and why I recommend certain tactics.

"Test, Launch, Scale" Framework

Everything LaunchBoom does boils down to "Test. Launch. Scale." This framework is the core strategy for building a long-term, successful business.

Here's how it breaks down.

PHASE 1: TEST

The core strategy of the test phase is validation of product demand during prelaunch. This is accomplished by testing product positioning and audience targeting in the market *before* you go to crowdfunding.

Companies that can test product ideas cheaply, quickly, and accurately can greatly reduce their risk, by launching only the products they know the market wants.

PHASE 2: LAUNCH

Products that pass the testing phase have the green light to launch through crowdfunding. The core strategy of the launch phase is to pre-sell a large amount of your product to the market. A combination of tactics will help you here:

- Build a community of people that want to buy your product *before* you launch.
- Hit your crowdfunding goal quickly – within the first twenty-four hours of the campaign.
- Rise to the top of the crowdfunding platform rankings and get free traffic.
- Continue momentum with qualified traffic from ads, email lists, and PR.
- Continue to pre-sell and upsell products to your backers once the campaign is over.

PHASE 3: SCALE

Once your product is manufactured and you have inventory on hand, you transition to the scale phase. The core strategy here is to build on your previous crowdfunding success and drive sales to your e-commerce website. Because you learned so much about marketing your product during the first two phases, you'll be able to scale your marketing efforts quickly.

The Framework Feeds on Itself

You can visualize the framework as shown below.

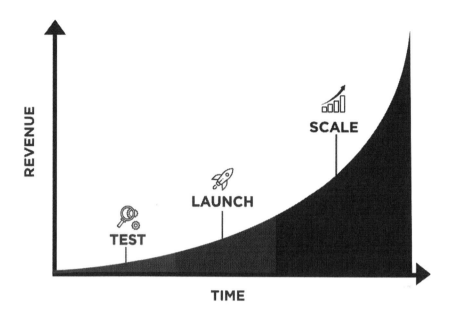

But I especially like to visualize it as a circle.

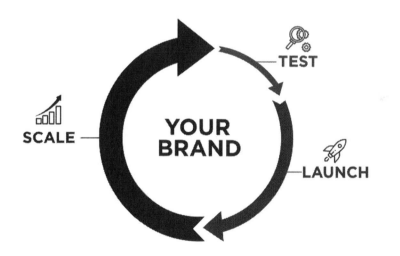

That's because the "test, launch, scale" framework is meant to feed on itself – and constantly grow your business.

Once you get to the scale phase, you can begin to work on the next product you want to test in the market. Ideally, you'll have multiple product ideas and be able test them against each other. You can choose the one with the best metrics during the test phase for the next product launch.

If you've successfully delivered a great experience throughout the entire process, you'll have a large group of happy customers who will support your next campaign. That's why we keep launching more products for our clients at LaunchBoom. We often see each campaign not only growing larger than the last, but becoming more profitable as well.

Using this framework, you'll be able to not only have a successful product launch, but you'll be well-positioned to build a successful brand.

Four Horsemen of Traffic

When I was getting started with crowdfunding, I would look at multi-million-dollar campaigns and wonder…

"Where is all this money coming from? The campaign creator must have a huge team focusing on hundreds of different sources of traffic to be able to raise this much money!"

Turns out I wasn't completely off-base. Typically, there are hundreds of sources that lead to sales, but the numbers might be a little misleading. When diving into those hundreds of sources, you'll realize that most of them belong to one of four distinct categories. And these four distinct categories make up the majority of all funds raised during campaigns.

I like to call them the **Four Horsemen of Traffic.**

Understanding who the Four Horsemen are makes planning your marketing strategy a lot easier. It allows you to focus on the areas that are going to bring you the most money, which will save you time, the most precious resource you have when planning your crowdfunding campaign.

Allow me to introduce you to The Four Horsemen of Traffic:

1. Your prelaunch email list
2. Online advertising
3. PR and influencer marketing
4. The crowdfunding platform

Now it's time for you to get to know each of these Horsemen a little more in depth.

Horseman #1: Your Prelaunch Email List

You build your prelaunch email list before your campaign launches, and it will consist of people interested in purchasing your product once you launch. There are many different ways to build a prelaunch email list, but my favorite is through Meta (Facebook) advertising.

This Horseman leads the charge. On average, we find that around 90 percent of the sales from the prelaunch email list will come within the first forty-eight hours. The goal of the prelaunch email list is to immediately drive sales to your campaign, once you launch. Ideally, the traffic from this Horseman alone will be enough to get your campaign funded.

Horseman #2: Online Advertising

Online advertising is a must for any crowdfunding campaign. And even with all the changes to ad tracking, the rise of TikTok, and all the damning headlines, Meta still reigns supreme. The return on investment (ROI) on other platforms (such as YouTube or TikTok, for example) don't come anywhere close to the ROI we see on Facebook and Instagram. So we tend to spend more than 90 percent of our ad budgets with Meta.

This Horseman will fight till the end. The online advertising Horseman will be with you for the remainder of the campaign (long after the prelaunch-email-list Horseman has retired). Consistent use of ads will allow you to keep sustained traffic throughout your campaign. Depending on how good the returns are, you can scale up and down as you please.

Horseman #3: PR and Influencer Marketing

Landing solid PR provides your campaign with two important things:

First, PR creates credibility. Everyone loves to see the "logo clouds" and comments from top media outlets.

Second, PR generates sales. Top-tier media placement can put millions of eyeballs on your product, which can drive tons of revenue.

As an example: Our campaign for BaKblade 2.0 got picked up by *Business Insider* in the last week of the campaign and proceeded to raise nearly $200K in four days.

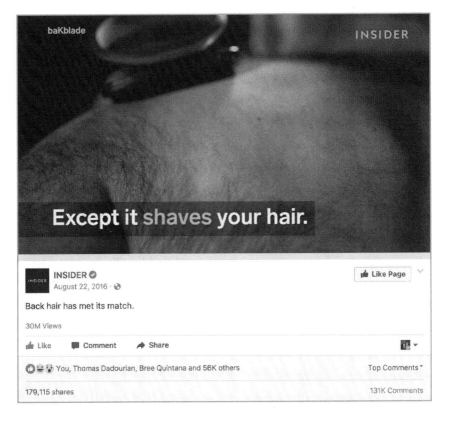

The original video that went viral received 30 million views (yes, 30 *million*), 56 thousand likes, 179,115 shares, and 131 thousand comments!

This Horseman fights in waves. Most of the time, the traffic you receive from PR and influencers will come in bursts. You'll get placement on a media site, see a spike in traffic and sales, and then see it die down just as fast. The good news is that PR placement tends to become easier to land with each placement you get.

Horseman #4: The Crowdfunding Platform

I'm always getting asked, "Why do you launch on Kickstarter or Indiegogo? Shouldn't you just launch on your own website so you have more control?" It's simple. There may be many reasons that crowdfunding platforms are the best place to launch your product, but the top reason has never changed — crowdfunding platforms have millions of visitors viewing their website every day. Tap into that traffic, and you'll raise a lot more money than you could otherwise.

This Horseman never rides alone. If the other three Horsemen don't show up to the campaign, then this Horseman won't appear either. Drive sales through your prelaunch email list, online advertising, and PR, and you'll start to see sales come in from the Kickstarter or Indiegogo communities, because both platforms have ranking systems. Generally, the more popular your campaign is, the higher you are in the rankings.

Fun fact: Last time I calculated the percentage of product sales from Kickstarter across all our campaigns, the number came out to 20 percent. That's a lot of sales!

Using This Information

Understanding this information and then using it is important because it will focus you on the sources of traffic that will drive the most sales to your campaign. There's a lot for you to keep on top of with your product launch. Figuring out where to put your time and your budget for promotions is extremely valuable. Instead of trying many ways to drive traffic, focus on these four, and it will pay off.

PART 2:
CREATING YOUR RESERVATION FUNNEL

CHAPTER

Launches are Won in the Prelaunch

"**I**f you build it, they will come."

You've probably heard this line before. It was inspired by the classic movie, *Field of Dreams*, when Ray Kinsella (Kevin Costner's character) hears a voice whisper, "If you build it, he will come." The "it" was a baseball field in the middle of a cornfield. And "he" was the character's dead father.

Ray builds it and, in true Hollywood fashion, his father comes (along with a whole team of long-deceased baseball players).

This line has been used ever since 1989 to inspire people to build their businesses and hold the belief that their customers will come.

The thing is, it's not that simple.

The phrase "if you build it, they will come" doesn't tell the whole story.

It really works like this:

If you build it, they will come, *only if* you get the prelaunch right.

You see, your crowdfunding campaign is like an island. And it's probably a really amazing island with a beach resort, ATV-ing, and all the amenities that someone could want. But the problem is that no one knows about that island or how to get there.

Your prelaunch is like a bridge.

It connects you with your potential customers and guides them to your crowdfunding campaign.

But it gets better. Once you build the first bridge to your island, and people start to see how amazing it is, other people will start to build their own bridges to your island.

My point is this: The entire success of your campaign depends on the prelaunch, and that's what most of this book is about.

Product Idea to Crowdfunded Framework

The Product Idea to Crowdfunded framework includes seven key milestones that must be completed to bring your product to life and become crowdfunded. Some milestones can only be completed once previous milestones have been addressed. Others can be worked on in parallel.

Let's examine each one now so you understand how they all work together.

MILESTONE #1: POSITIONING

Great product positioning is the foundation on which the rest of your crowdfunding campaign is built. If your product positioning is shaky at the start, your whole campaign will collapse before you finish.

So, what is great product positioning?

Great product positioning means you are effectively communicating the value of your product to your target audience. There are two key ideas you need to understand here:

1. You'll need to find your **target audience**: How do you locate the people online who experience the problem that your product solves?
2. You'll need to be good at **communicating the value**: It's critical to explain how your product solves their problem.

I'll teach you how to use the Consumer-Based Brand Equity (CBBE) framework to build strong positioning.

MILESTONE #2: PRODUCT IMAGERY

Once you know how you want to position your product, it's time to create assets for use in marketing. That's more than just taking a pretty picture.

You've got to capture your product in ways that communicate your unique selling points. You want your potential customers to *see* themselves using your product.

I'll teach you how to create assets that not only look good, but make people want to buy your product.

MILESTONE #3: RESERVATION FUNNEL

Building a prelaunch email list is the most important ingredient of a successful launch. It's not as easy as just throwing up a landing page and collecting email addresses.

For example, how do you know if the people giving you their email addresses actually want to buy your product?

We asked that highly crucial question when we first started Launch-Boom. The answer led us to create the LaunchBoom reservation funnel.

Instead of only collecting emails, we also allow people to place a deposit (of at least $1) to reserve the best deal on the launch. We've found that people who put down a deposit are *thirty times more likely* to buy than someone who just provides their email address.

I'll teach you how to create the LaunchBoom reservation funnel.

MILESTONE #4: ADS LIVE

Once you have your reservation funnel, you need to send traffic to start building your prelaunch email list. The best way to do that is through advertising.

As you already know, Meta's platform (Facebook and Instagram) reigns supreme. That's why most clients spend 100 percent of their ad budgets for the prelaunch on Meta.

I'll teach you our entire advertising strategy so you can set it up for yourself.

MILESTONE #5: CAMPAIGN PAGE

Your campaign page is one of the two most important creative assets for your launch. This is the landing page that everyone will see when they navigate to your Kickstarter or Indiegogo campaign.

At this point, you'll have learned so much from building your prelaunch list through advertising that you'll be able to take your learnings and apply what you know to your campaign page.

We're going to delve into how to write your copy and design a high-converting campaign page.

MILESTONE #6: CAMPAIGN VIDEO

Your campaign video, the one everyone will see when they land on your Kickstarter or Indiegogo campaign, is the second of the two most important creative assets for your launch.

To be clear, your campaign video is really an advertisement. The main goal is to turn viewers into buyers.

I'll teach you how to write a script that sells and get your video affordably produced.

MILESTONE #7: LAUNCH

This is it: All your hard work has led to this point. It's time to push the launch button!

With everything else complete, this part will be easy. You'll use your prelaunch email list to drive traffic and get funded on the first day. From there, building on your early success will be simple.

I'll teach you how to launch – and how to use your prelaunch email list to get funded the first day.

Build a Strong Foundation

It bears repeating: launches are won in the prelaunch. And winning the prelaunch can be accomplished by following the "Product Idea to Crowdfunded" framework. Each step builds on another, which means that you have to execute well on each milestone to realize a successful launch.

That means there's no skipping anything!

Now, let's go to one of the keystones of the foundation: product positioning. Do that right and everything else will be much easier.

CHAPTER 7

Building the Foundation Through Product Positioning

It's surprising, but 59 percent of all crowdfunding campaigns fail. When I tell people this, most are shocked and then immediately ask…

"Why?"

Well, the answer usually leaves them more shocked.

The answer is: They didn't position their product correctly.

That's right. The number one reason that products don't succeed is poor product positioning. Great product positioning is essential for the foundation on which the rest of a successful crowdfunding campaign is built. But start with weak product positioning, and your whole campaign will topple over before you finish.

Case in point: When I say Old Spice, what comes to mind?

Probably their hilarious and crazy commercials. But many people don't remember that Old Spice's positioning used to be quite different.

A long time ago, the brand appealed to an older male demographic, but by the 2000s they were seeing sales decline rapidly. They knew they had a great product, but they needed to change their positioning.

In 2010, they made their new positioning public with the release of their first commercial, "The Man Your Man Could Smell Like." The ad quickly became a viral sensation, particularly among the younger, internet-savvy audience that Old Spice was trying to capture.

Old Spice did nothing to change their product. All they did was change how they *positioned* their product. And the result: Sales increased by 125 percent – showing just how powerful positioning can be.

What Makes Great Product Positioning?

Great product positioning means effectively communicating the value of your product to your target audience. As I mentioned earlier, it involves having a lock on two key aspects:

1. **Target audience:** the people who experience the problem that your product solves
2. **Communicating the value:** explaining how your product solves their problem

For brand-new products, which yours is, developing great product positioning is a process that takes time. You may think you already know how to communicate the value effectively and who your target audience is, but any initial ideas you have are pure hypotheses...and are probably wrong.

It's important to know this when developing your product positioning, because you shouldn't be deeply attached to any of your initial ideas. Everything should be approached with an open mind, and you should be ready and willing to test different ways to position your product and listen to the market tell you which is best.

Let's dive into a framework we use at LaunchBoom to come up with initial product positioning.

The Consumer-Based Brand Equity Pyramid

At this point, your product is probably somewhere between an idea and a functional prototype. Any thought of who your customers will be and what product positioning they will respond to is purely a hypothesis, so far.

First, we need to get all of this information out of your head and into writing.

To do this, I'll be showing you the Consumer-Based Brand Equity (CBBE) pyramid, a product positioning framework we use at Launch-Boom. I've found this to be lean enough that it doesn't take too much time to complete, yet powerful enough to have a profound impact on any campaign.

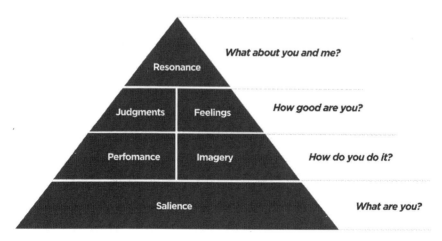

Scan the QR code or go to <u>crowdfundedbook.com/positioning</u> and download the *Product Positioning Worksheet* to follow along.

The underlying principle of CBBE is the assumption that you do not own your brand, but rather, consumers do. It's a concept to them, something that lives rent-free in their minds. For that reason, we approach product positioning as if we are the consumer.

The framework is visualized as a pyramid, and it's best to read it from bottom to top. Doing so tells the story of a consumer's relationship with a brand, and each subsequent tier builds on the one(s) below it. Consumers may develop thoughts and feelings that belong in every box in the CBBE pyramid in a single second, but time-wise, they will still run from bottom to top.

To illustrate how this framework works, let's try an experiment. I'm going to give you the name of a brand you most likely know. I want you to notice what appears in your mind's eye – what images, associations, sensations, and experiences come to you? Here we go…

Starbucks.

Okay, your brain has already gone through the entire framework in the blink of an eye. Here's how it works for me:

- **Salience:** sells coffee
- **Performance:** affordable, locations everywhere, fast, easy experience, same coffee every time
- **Imagery:** green mermaid logo, cozy coffee shop, coffee with cream

- **Judgments:** consistent, friendly staff, coffee tastes decent
- **Feelings:** warmth, caffeine buzz, trustworthy, dependable, loyal
- **Resonance:** will choose Starbucks and go with friends and family because I trust the company and consistent experience I'm assured of

You may have completely different associations with Starbucks, but I'll bet you relate to quite a few of the thoughts I had. Starbucks has spent *a lot* of time and money for me to have those associations with their brand.

Even though you're just beginning the process, you can still design how you want your consumer to think and feel about your brand. Let's start with the base of the pyramid.

Level 1: What are you?

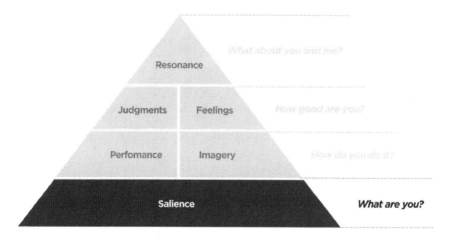

Level 1 is salience, the foundation of the pyramid, which means something like significance, or obviousness. In this context, it refers to what would be considered the most pertinent aspects of a product. During this level, the consumer is asking the broad question, "What are you?" If your brand has salience, the consumer knows who you are and what problem you solve.

The best way to establish salience is to state, in the simplest way possible, what problem you solve. You'll want to use words and broad associations that consumers will recognize, so that they can quickly associate your product with a category they already understand.

Do not overthink this part!

For example, let's talk about our campaign, the Give'r Frontier Mittens, which raised $1,356,709 on Kickstarter and Indiegogo InDemand. Our headline was "The Best Damn Mittens Ever." The "mittens" part plays to salience. We could have gone with "the quad-layer, super-warm, hand insulator" instead, but we didn't choose that.

Why not?

Because no one knows what that means. They can probably pull some associations from that language and they might think it sounds cool, but if they aren't 100 percent sure what you are, then that's a fail.

Level 2: How do you do it?

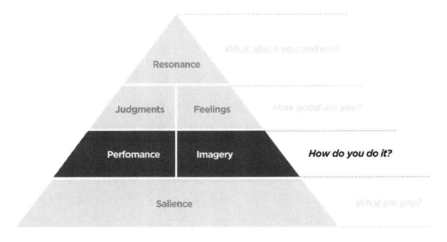

The next level of the pyramid is about *performance* and *imagery*. At this stage, the consumer is asking, "How do you do it?" This is where they're trying to understand what makes you different from the competition. Let's look at these two elements.

PERFORMANCE

Some questions you need to answer about performance are:

- What makes you different from your competition? (This is called "points of difference.")
- What makes you similar to your competition? (This is called "points of parity.")
- What are the core features of your product?
- How valuable is your product?

As an example, let's talk about our campaign, LoftTek, which raised $1,041,308 on Kickstarter and Indiegogo InDemand. Here's a graphic we used that plays entirely to performance:

In our graphic, consumers see all the primary features of the jacket with certain features highlighted. It illustrates the points of parity and points of difference. For example, many jackets have zipper pockets, a hood, water resistance, and more, and consumers love these features. But not many jackets have *all* these features.

The fact that LoftTek is over-engineered is not only a feature, it's a point of difference. This is the level of detail you'll want to describe in your questionnaire.

In the end, the main goal of answering these questions is to identify how your product performs better than the competition's. Ideally, you'll have three main points of difference.

IMAGERY

Some questions that you'll need to answer about imagery are:

- What brands would you associate with your product?
- Where is your product used?
- How is your product used?

Our campaign for William Painter Empire Sunglasses, which raised $865,235 on Kickstarter and Indiegogo InDemand, helps illustrate this. We imagined their product being used outdoors in exciting locations. We also wanted to associate the brand with one that was high-tech, adventurous, and innovative. That's why we chose NASA.

Our top-performing headline in ads was "These NASA Inspired Sunglasses Are Made Of Aerospace-Grade Titanium." Below, you can see our best-performing ad, which captured exactly what we came up with during the positioning process.

WILLIAMPAINTER.COM
These NASA Inspired Sunglasses Are Made Of Aerospace-Grade Titanium

824   154 Comments 211 Shares

The performance and imagery sections of the pyramid will most influence your photography and video. Identify where you think people will use your product. Then, capture imagery in those locations.

Level 3: How good are you?

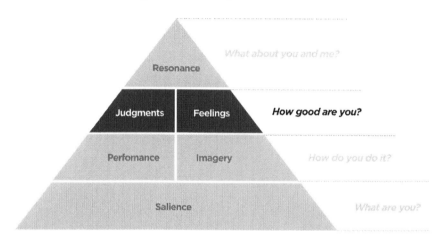

The next level of the pyramid is made of *judgments* and *feelings*. At this point, the consumer is asking the question, "How good are you?" Essentially, the consumer is trying to figure out what they think and feel about your brand/product. They're taking your performance and imagery points from the layer below, evaluating them, and forming opinions about them.

JUDGMENTS

Some questions to answer here are:

- What positive judgments will people have about your product?
- What concerns or doubts might people have about your product?
- What credibility do you have in this space?

In our campaign for the Neck Hammock, which raised $1,642,934 on Kickstarter and Indiegogo InDemand, we claimed it could offer neck pain relief in ten minutes or less.

We knew that this would cause some people concern and doubt, with questions such as:

- Is there scientific evidence of why it works?
- What's the credibility of the person who created it?
- Are there testimonials from people who have used it?

Each of these concerns, and many more, were directly addressed in our messaging. For example:

- Is there scientific evidence of why it works?
  - We explained the science of cervical traction and how it works.
- What's the credibility of the person who created it?
  - The founder is a doctor and licensed physical therapist who used the device on his patients.
- Are there testimonials from people who have used it?
  - We included written and video testimonials from the founder's clients.

Here's a graphic from Neck Hammock's campaign page:

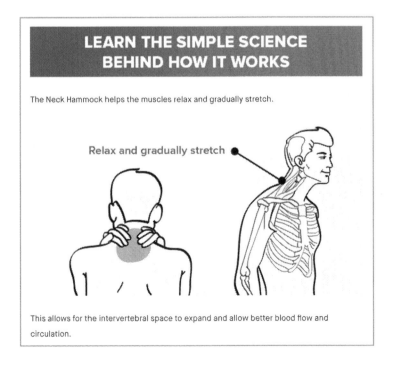

LEARN THE SIMPLE SCIENCE BEHIND HOW IT WORKS

The Neck Hammock helps the muscles relax and gradually stretch.

Relax and gradually stretch

This allows for the intervertebral space to expand and allow better blood flow and circulation.

Because we took the time to identify possible negative judgments before we launched, we were able to address any concerns, doubts, or questions of credibility directly within our messaging.

FEELINGS

Some questions that you'll answer about feelings are:

- How do you want people to feel when using your product?
- What is the voice of your message? (Is it the voice of a friend, a teacher, a doctor, a professional, an expert, and what type of language will we be using?)
- What's the tone of your message? (Funny, somber, optimistic, epic, intense, friendly, etc.)

AIR PIX, which raised $1,611,851 on Indiegogo, is an aerial drone that allows you to take photo and video selfies. Our campaign sought to capture feelings of youthfulness and fun. When thinking this through, we knew that the word "drone" just did *not* convey those feelings. Most consumers associate drones with tech-focused brands or the military – not the mental imagery we wanted the potential consumer to associate with AIR PIX.

So we decided to drop the word "drone" from our messaging. Instead, we called AIR PIX an "aerial camera" and our most popular headline was "Your Pocket-Sized Aerial Photographer." Even though it technically *is* a drone, we found another way to describe what AIR PIX is without using that word.

Level 4: What about you and me?

We've made it to the top of the pyramid! The only thing left to cover is resonance. At this stage, the consumer is asking the question, "What about you and me?" This is where we identify reasons the consumer will enjoy a loyal, active relationship with your brand.

Some questions that you'll answer concerning resonance include:

- Why would you be missed if your product suddenly disappeared off the market?
- How is your mission in alignment with your customer's mission?
- Why will your customers only choose you?

Our campaign for etee, which raised $380,641 on Indiegogo, leaned heavily into resonance. A membership club for people who want plastic-free alternatives to everyday items, etee's mission is to remove plastic from our world. This is a massive goal, but one that their audience can get behind.

But resonance isn't only about having an altruistic mission. In fact, most brands don't have a massive, world-changing mission, and that's okay!

Let's go back to the Starbucks example. At the end of the day, they make and serve coffee. Now, I love coffee, but the world doesn't need it in the same way we need to reduce our plastic consumption. Still, Starbucks has been able to build an extremely loyal and active customer base.

How?

Because resonance is about more than an altruistic mission. It's about *anything* that creates loyalty between the customer and the brand. For

Starbucks, this includes things like loyalty programs and creating a sense of belonging in their stores.

In the long-term, resonance is most important. But for most product creators with brand-new companies, it isn't going to be the reason people buy. That's important to remember when spending your valuable time coming up with your positioning.

Developing Your Product Positioning

Go to crowdfundedbook.com/positioning and download the *Product Positioning Worksheet*. Answer each question as completely as possible. If you feel stuck, you may be overthinking the question. It shouldn't take more than two hours. The following information will guide you through filling it out.

SECTION 1: CBBE QUESTIONNAIRE

In the first section of the worksheet, we break down each part of the CBBE Questionnaire and have specific questions for you. Answer every question as completely as possible. When I do this kind of thing, I've often found it helpful to use bulleted lists so I can get an abundance of ideas down in writing.

SECTION 2: TARGET MARKET

Once the questionnaire is complete, it's time to identify who you think your target market is — the people who will actually want to buy your product.

For this part, you'll identify the top three audiences you believe will be most interested in your product. Here's an example:

Audience #1: Snowsport enthusiast

Age range: 25-44

Gender: Male/female

Interests: Atomic skis, Fischer, snowboard, cross-country skiing, Snowboard Magazine, Freeskiing, Transworld Snowboarding, Freeskier Magazine, backcountry skiing, ski mountaineering, alpine skiing, freestyle skiing, Burton snowboards

Geographic location: United States

The defined audiences are going to come in especially handy when we get to the advertising portion of your prelaunch.

SECTION 3: VALUE POSITIONING

With the questions answered and possible audiences identified, you're ready to distill your answers into more focused, usable messaging.

The first step in value positioning is identifying your top three differentiators. Essentially, how is your product *way* better than what already exists? If you don't have at least one differentiator that shows you're much better than the competition, you probably shouldn't launch.

The second step in value positioning is to identify your headlines. For this, I like to envision the crowdfunding campaign page, which will have a headline and a subheadline for any product. Written well, they are able to communicate the value of your product very simply.

Your Foundation Is Set

You've completed the first milestone! Congrats on getting through most people's least favorite part of the process!

Remember, it's important to note that your initial product positioning is pure hypothesis. Nailing your product positioning is an iterative process that requires testing. Stay open and get ready for the current positioning to be challenged and changed.

Now – it's time to build the assets you need to start your prelaunch.

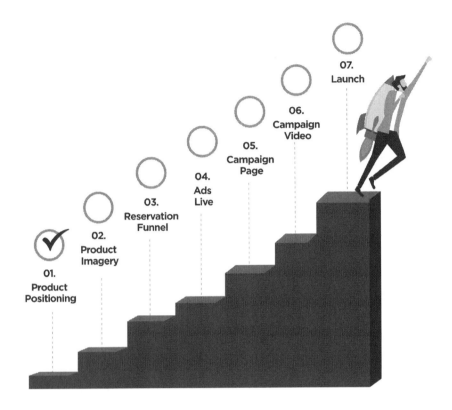

CHAPTER

Capturing Product Imagery

Product imagery takes your positioning and makes it come to life visually. Every feature, benefit, and use case will be captured. From your ads to your campaign page, the images you capture will be used across your entire campaign.

That's why you have to take the time to get it right. But don't worry, that doesn't mean it's incredibly difficult to do.

There are two types of product imagery: photorealistic renderings and photography. We'll cover both and get into the nitty-gritty of how to do it right.

Photorealistic Renderings

As the name suggests, photorealistic renderings are natural-looking images of your product that are created by a computer. They're used everywhere in marketing, and you probably see them every day without even noticing. They're super-useful for that reason.

61

Typically, you can make them more quickly and more affordably than professionally taken photos. Plus, since they're made with a computer, you have a lot of control over your product's appearance, from materials used to lighting and environment. This allows you to create the exact image you want.

It's worth noting that photorealistic renderings are *not* allowed on Kickstarter and they *are* allowed on Indiegogo. (That doesn't mean I recommend Indiegogo, by the way... just an FYI.) Even though the renderings aren't useful for a Kickstarter campaign, they're still useful.

Many clients create photorealistic renderings even when their prototype isn't photo-ready. With the renderings, they can start their prelaunch marketing efforts while finishing their prototype. Eventually, they'll get the real photos, but the renderings can speed up the launch process.

THEY WORK

I need to shatter a myth about photorealistic renderings. It's a common misconception that photorealistic renderings won't perform well in marketing campaigns, based on a mistaken idea that consumers will prefer real images and decide not to buy.

We've launched three campaigns that used 100 percent photorealistic renderings. Yes, that's right. There was not one real photo used in any of these three campaigns for boutique hotels that were launched on Indiegogo (again, because Kickstarter doesn't allow photorealistic renderings). Combined, we drove $2,635,782 in presale revenue for these three campaigns.

This example is for Bubble Hotels, the first hotel we launched.

I'm not telling you this to encourage you to (1) launch on Indiegogo or (2) only use photorealistic renderings. I just want you to see that photorealistic renderings are capable of driving millions in revenue.

GETTING THEM MADE

This is one of the few areas where I'm not going to teach you how to do it yourself. To be honest, creating photorealistic renderings is beyond me. We always hire a 3D render artist to get them made because they're affordable – usually in the ballpark of $750.

A simple Google search will show you that there are lots of 3D render artists out there. However, choosing the *right* artist can be overwhelming. I recommend:

1. **Upwork,** the biggest freelancer marketplace. Put up a job posting and you could be working with a 3D render artist in 24 hours.
2. **LaunchBoom Experts,** where we keep a list of vetted contractors and companies that we've worked with extensively. Clients get discounted rates.

Before you choose your 3D render artist, here are a few things you'll need:

1. **Design files:** Provide any design files or drawings that have been created for your product. These can be in the form of CAD files, or even sketches.
2. **Shot list:** Make a list of different renderings you'll want created. At a minimum, I suggest that you create renderings from the same angles as your studio-style photography (we'll discuss that in a minute). You can also ask for renderings to be created in "lifestyle" settings.
3. **Reference material:** Provide a folder with images of other products that you'd like to emulate. This will make it way easier to have a conversation with the render artist.

Photorealistic renderings are not required, but they can be very helpful. Use them to quickly generate images for marketing or complement the real photos you already have.

Product Photography

Now let's talk about the real stuff: product photography. Unless you're launching a boutique hotel, every campaign will need this. Let's dive into the specifics.

STUDIO

Studio-style product photos are the "glamour shots" of your product, highlighting every angle and feature. They are typically shot against a plain background and make your product the focus of the image.

These photos typically require a higher level of skill and equipment. That's why I recommend hiring a professional. (More on that later.)

The two categories of studio shots you'll want to capture are:

1. Whole Product

These are studio photos of the whole product, but at differing angles.

- Straight-on
- 45-degree angle
- Profile
- Back

This example of studio shots is from our campaign for Author Clock, which raised $2,217,773 on Kickstarter and Indiegogo InDemand:

2. Features

Take close-up shots of each key feature, ideally between two and five, total.

Here's an example of feature shots from our campaign, Scorpio Pizza Oven, which raised $101,225 on Indiegogo:

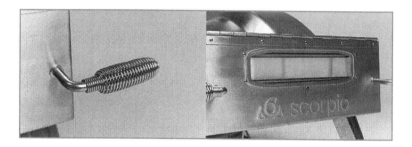

LOCATION

Location photos showcase your product in the environment where it's intended to be used. You want to give potential customers a taste of what it's like to own and use your product.

The most important questions to ask here are:

1. Who will use my product?
2. Where will they use my product?

Since you've already gone through the product positioning process, you should have these questions answered!

Aim for two or three different environments that capture different use cases and audiences. The shots should focus on the product, but keep the shots relatively wide so you can see the background and space it lives in.

This location shot is from our campaign for Gryphon, which raised $142,744 on Indiegogo.

ACTION

Action shots are useful for features that are better showcased through motion or interaction.

Focus on the exact action or feature you want to showcase. Eliminate anything that distracts from that feature and make sure you can clearly see what's happening in the shot.

Action shots can be videos, too. For example, our campaign for the Pepper Cannon, which raised $3,017,654 on Kickstarter and Indiegogo InDemand, claimed that it could pepper a steak in seven cranks instead of seventy. Showing that feature using a quick video was way more effective than a photo could have been.

Still photos can be good, too. Here's an example of an action photo for our campaign, Tandem Shower, which raised $774,113 on Kickstarter:

CAPTURING YOUR PHOTOS

Even though it's possible to capture amazing photos using your phone, most people hire professional photographers, and they don't have to be super expensive. Most creators I've worked with know a professional photographer who will take the photos and videos for an affordable price.

Now You Have Your Product Images

Your product images are critical to the rest of your prelaunch marketing strategy. And now that they're finished, you've completed another milestone!

You're now ready to build your reservation funnel! This is my favorite part of the whole process, as we start building the prelaunch email list that you'll use to get funded the first day.

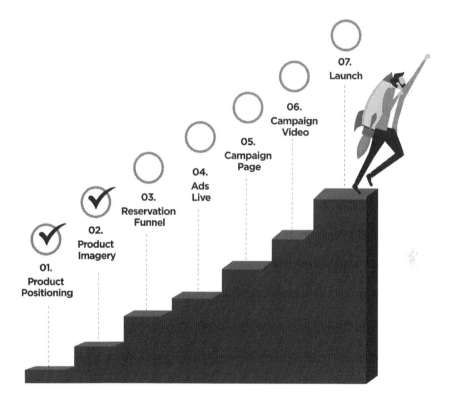

CHAPTER

How to Build Your Reservation Funnel

Since LaunchBoom's inception in 2015, building a highly qualified prelaunch email list has been a key part of our launch strategy. The prelaunch email list is how we get our clients funded in the first 24 hours – which we call having a "LaunchBoom." Flash forward to 2017, when we started experimenting with a change to our prelaunch strategy that *transformed the entire crowdfunding industry.*

You see, the challenge with building a prelaunch email list is measuring how qualified it is—and by qualified, I mean how likely email subscribers are to buy your product when you launch the crowdfunding campaign.

For our first two years, we wrestled with this question, with little luck. I even hired a data scientist to look at all our campaigns and try to find correlations between prelaunch metrics (like cost per lead, email open rate, lead-to-reach ratio) and the likelihood that customers would buy.

The short and disappointing answer: the data scientist couldn't find any strong correlation.

It all changed one seemingly normal day, when Rebecca, one of our video editors, sent me a link to a product she liked. The creators weren't launching a crowdfunding campaign, but they were taking $1 deposits on their website. Anyone who put down a $1 deposit was reserving the product at the best discount once it launched.

I knew immediately that this simple idea was something big. I contacted the founder of that project, who graciously shared the strategy behind the $1 reservation. He felt it was a better way to build a prelaunch email list. The top reasons are:

1. Making a purchase on a website (even for only one dollar) is a much better indicator of purchase intent than just giving your email address.
2. By tracking the $1 deposits, you can optimize advertisements for people who've made $1 deposits versus leads.

Within a week, we started testing this strategy for our clients and began to see results almost immediately. That was back in early 2017. Since that time, we've learned a lot and fine-tuned the funnel accordingly.

How the Reservation Funnel Works

Even though our reservation funnel is quite simple to understand, getting all the pieces to work well together has taken a long time and a lot of testing. Here's a blueprint of what it looks like:

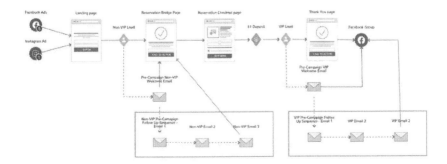

Complicated, you think? No, it's not so bad – you'll see as I go into each step of the funnel in detail. I'll be using examples from our Bonc Bike campaign, which raised £665,368 on Indiegogo (note, that's in pounds, not dollars).

STEP 1: AD

The user clicks on a Facebook or Instagram ad and is taken to a landing page.

STEP 2: LANDING PAGE SIGN-UP

The landing page includes a simple call to action: providing an email address, so they can get notified when we launch.

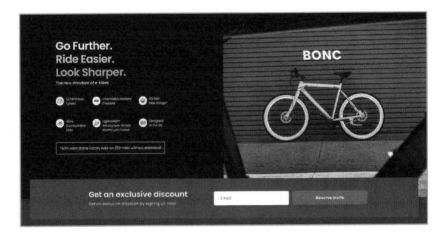

STEP 3: RESERVATION BRIDGE

After providing an email address, we thank the user and make them an offer: They can put down a $1 deposit to become a "VIP" and reserve the best deal we'll have at launch. There is no checkout on this page, which is why we call it a "bridge."

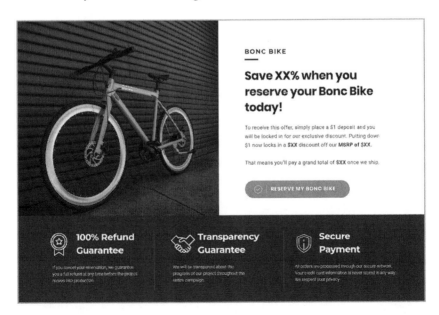

We've found that adding this step between the initial landing page and the checkout increases the conversion rate. Having the checkout on this page would be jarring for the visitor. They aren't expecting it, so it comes across as too promotional.

Instead, we thank them for signing up and explain the opportunity to become a VIP. If they want to, they can press a button to be taken to the checkout page.

STEP 4: RESERVATION CHECKOUT

If they click on the button to reserve the product, they are taken to a checkout page where they can complete their reservation.

STEP 5: THANK YOU

Once they check out, they're taken to a simple "thank you" page. We recommend creating an exclusive group they can join and adding a button to that page. Most of our clients create a VIP-only Facebook group, but Discord is popular as well.

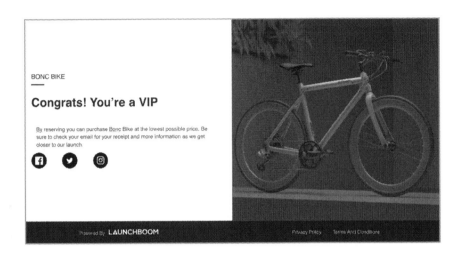

STEP 6: WELCOME EMAIL AUTOMATION

The last step occurs in parallel with some of the previous steps. When someone signs up for your email list, you will enter them into automated email sequences.

In the next chapter I'll go into more detail on setting this up.

The Difference Between VIPs and Non-VIPs

The entire point of the reservation funnel is to collect leads. But not all the leads are the same. We have two categories of leads:

1. **VIPs:** people who put down at least a $1 deposit to reserve your product
2. **Non-VIPs:** people who don't put down a deposit to reserve your product

I'll continue to use these terms, VIP and non-VIP, to describe these two different segments. Understanding the differences between these two groups is extremely important to the success of your campaign.

VIPS ARE 30x MORE LIKELY TO PURCHASE

Having used our reservation funnel since 2017, we've been able to collect some amazing data on its effectiveness.

Here's the most important stat: VIPs are *thirty times more likely to purchase* when we launch than non-VIPs.

That statistic is an average – I've seen it both higher and lower. For example, on our campaign for the OGarden Smart, the VIPs were *sixty times* more likely to purchase than the non-VIPs. We generated $129,820 from the prelaunch email list alone, and went on to raise a total of $739,187 on Kickstarter.

Simply put, the reservation funnel allows you to:

- Optimize your advertisements for purchase intent versus lead intent.
- Allocate your ad budget more effectively and get a higher *return on ad spend* (ROAS).
- Build a community of people who are thirty times more likely to buy your product when you launch.

Now that you know how important VIPs are, let's look at building your reservation funnel.

Creating Your VIP Offer

Your VIP offer is what people will get by putting down a deposit to upgrade to VIP. There are a few ways to structure this so it will be very enticing.

However you choose to structure your VIP offer, though, the most important thing is for it to feel *exclusive*. You want to appeal to your potential customer in a way that makes them feel this is a special event – it's got to be worth it for someone to pull out their credit card and give you money before you've even launched.

Here are a few ideas for VIP offers that I've seen work well.

VIP OFFER #1: GUARANTEED BEST DISCOUNT

The most common VIP offer is a guarantee of the best discount. By upgrading to VIP, buyers are assured that when you launch, they'll be given the best deal.

For example, on our Give'r Frontier Mittens campaign, which raised $1,356,709 on Kickstarter and Indiegogo InDemand, this was the VIP offer:

Save 41% by putting down a $1 deposit now.

This was the reservation bridge page:

"Guaranteed best offer" is a great choice for any product, and I'd especially advise it for anyone in the tech or design categories.

VIP OFFER #2: EXCLUSIVE ADD-ON

The second most common VIP offer is an exclusive add-on. Instead of a discount, you're giving the customer a different value-based offer: something additional if they purchase your product when you launch.

For example, on our campaign for Alpha Clash Trading Card Game, which raised $422,809 on Kickstarter, the VIP offer was this:

Get two exclusive trading cards by putting down a $10 deposit now.

Here's their reservation bridge page:

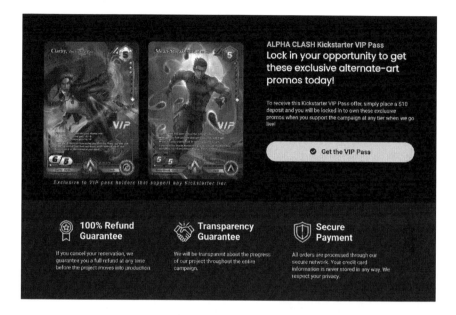

I'd advise going with this VIP offer if you're in the gaming category. But again, this offer can work in many categories.

VIP OFFER #3: FIRST CHOICE

In some cases, giving VIPs the first opportunity to experience your product is a huge value-add for them. This is particularly useful when whatever you're offering is going to be very scarce.

For example, our client Mirror Hotels, who raised $1,716,192 on Indiegogo, had this VIP offer:

Get 50% off and first access to the booking page by putting down a $50 deposit.

Their reservation bridge page showing that offer is here:

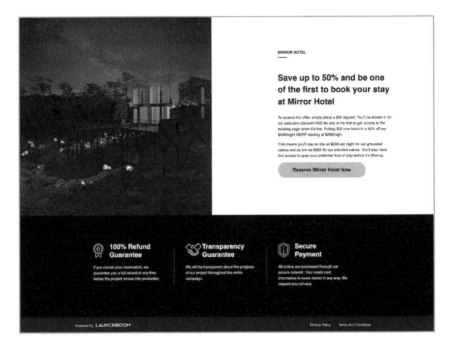

If you're in the lodging category, I'd advise this VIP offer. But again, it also works across many categories.

ADDITIONAL VIP PERK

Whichever VIP offer you choose to present, there's an additional perk that I recommend adding. If someone upgrades to VIP, you should invite them into a VIP-only community. The VIP-only community is a place where VIPs can communicate directly with your team and with each other.

This has a lot of utility leading up to the launch, but many of our clients continue nurturing this community post-launch. If you do it well, you'll create a hyper-engaged community that you can leverage for product feedback, beta testing, driving traffic to new products, and much more.

The most common platform I've used for this is a good ol' Facebook group. But we also use Discord if the audience is more comfortable with that. Especially in the gaming community where users love Discord, it's much more effective than Facebook groups.

Here's an example of the VIP Facebook group for our campaign for the Top Shelf Camera Bag, which raised $1,014,422 on Kickstarter. The VIPs-only group has 839 members.

And here's an example of the VIP Discord group for our campaign, Alpha Clash, which has 602 members.

Welcome Email Automation

Once you start building your prelaunch email list, you must have a communications strategy in place.

I think of your email list like a houseplant, which will wither away if left alone. And on the flip side, there is such a thing as "over-watering" your email list, too. You've got to find the sweet spot between too little and too much communication.

THE STRATEGY

When someone signs up for your email list, you want to welcome them immediately using email automation, with the welcome messages differentiated for VIPs and non-VIPs. Within your email marketing software, you can set up an automated email to be delivered to new subscribers to your email list. In this case, you'll want to set up two automations: one for VIPs, and a different one for non-VIPs.

For VIPs, you'll be introducing yourself as well as reminding them of the benefits of being on the VIP list.

For non-VIPs, you'll also be introducing yourself, but the main call to action will be to get them to upgrade to VIP.

Make sure the email account you're sending your email marketing messages from is an account you're monitoring. You should expect people to respond to your email marketing, and that's a chance for you to start a one-to-one conversation with your list. This is a good thing. It allows you to begin to form a relationship with your community, which will make them more likely to buy.

Download our *Welcome Emails Template* to make this easier for you. Scan the QR code or go to crowdfundedbook.com/email.

PERSONALIZE YOUR EMAILS

It's important to give your emails a personal touch. People like to interact with other people, not a generic brand message. That means you'll want your emails to be sent from *you*.

As an example, if I'm sending an email from my company, Launch-Boom, I'd have the "from" name be "Mark at LaunchBoom" instead of just "LaunchBoom." All the copy within the email will be as if I personally am writing to the email subscriber one-to-one, rather than addressing the list as a group.

Putting It All Together

That was a lot of essential information in this chapter, and you may want to review it later. For now, though, you have what you need for a full understanding of why the reservation funnel is so powerful, and how to set it up.

That means you've completed milestone #3! Congrats!

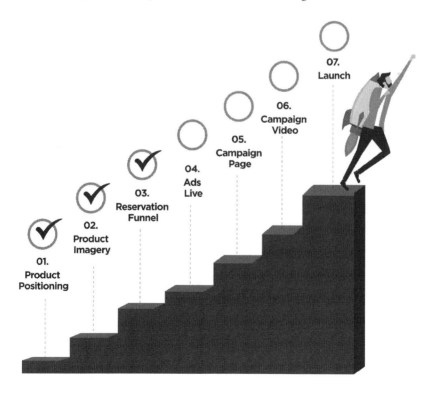

If you're feeling overwhelmed, take a breath and let me reassure you – you've got this! In the chapter titled "30-Day Reservation Funnel Challenge," I'll provide you with tons of free resources to build your funnel.

Next, you'll learn how to send traffic to your reservation funnel so you can start to build an email list that's thirty times more likely to buy.

PART 3:
BUILDING YOUR PRELAUNCH EMAIL LIST

CHAPTER

Driving Traffic with Paid Ads

With your reservation funnel set up, the fun part begins. It's time to start driving traffic to build your prelaunch email list. I've found that once you get your first email sign-up, everything will start to feel more *real*. Wow – a real person wants to know about your product! That excitement and momentum will carry you through to your launch.

The most effective way to build your prelaunch email list is by using Meta (Facebook/Instagram) advertising. Yes, Meta still reigns supreme for lead generation, and I doubt it's going to change for many years. I've found Meta ads to be the most dependable, cost-effective, and scalable way to build an email list.

That doesn't mean you can't use other methods to drive traffic to your reservation funnel, but Meta advertising should be your primary focus.

When it comes to Meta advertising, you may hear people talk about how complex it is to do it right. Don't let them fool you. There are only three things that you have to get right for Meta ads to work:

1. Target the right audience
2. Create attention-grabbing imagery
3. Write engaging copy

Let's start with the most important part: targeting.

Getting Targeting Right

If you target the wrong people, you'll never hit your desired metrics. Or worse…you'll waste your money and build an unqualified list that doesn't convert.

Meta's user data is mind-blowing. With *over 3.7 billion* monthly active users as of 2023, their options for targeting are extensive. It can be overwhelming to start.

So let's start with a simple exercise.

CREATE YOUR DREAM 20

Tomorrow, twenty brands of your choosing will be sending out an email to all of their customers promoting your product.

Think about it: If this were the actual scenario, which twenty brands would you choose to promote your product?

Make a list of twenty people, brands, organizations, or communities that you wish would send an email on your behalf. If you went through the Product Positioning Worksheet, you've already done some of this work when you identified your top three audiences.

Here are some quick tips to help you with your choices:

- People, brands, organizations, communities, and Facebook pages are all okay, but interests, such as "running" or "eating healthy," don't qualify.
- You want to choose groups that have spent a significant amount of time and energy building their communities. Use all of their efforts – they did the hard work for you already.
- Be selective. You want to choose audiences that include a large percentage of people who would convert. For example, if you

have a cool nerdy product that was featured on *Good Morning America* you might get a ton of views, but sales might only come from a small percentage of that audience. Going after TechCrunch would be a much better choice.

▪ The targets shouldn't be too small. If they are too small (fewer than 25k-50k fans) you won't be able to target them on Meta.

Here's one more brainstorming framework we love to use. We call it the Four F's framework. Ask yourself the following questions to come up with more specific interests to target.

1. Who does your market *follow*?

What specific influencers or people does your audience follow? Instead of targeting "entrepreneurs," target Gary Vaynerchuk, Tim Ferriss, Fast Company, and so on.

2. Where does your audience *frequent*?

Where do they spend their time? Instead of targeting "fitness," target 24-Hour Fitness, Ironman, CrossFit Games, etc.

3. What do they do for *fun*?

What activities does your audience like? Instead of targeting "outdoors," target hiking, backpacking, camping, etc.

4. What particular products do they *fund*?

What do they spend their money on? Instead of targeting "running," target Adidas, FitBit, RoadRunner, etc.

If there's overlap between your answers, that's totally fine! This is simply a tool to help you brainstorm different interests for your Dream 20.

Once your Dream 20 list is finished, it's time to build your audiences in Facebook. We recommend two basic types of audiences:

▪ **Interest audiences** — using your Dream 20 and Meta's suggestion engine, generate a large list of targets.

▪ **Lookalike audiences** — use existing audiences/email lists and have Meta generate a similar audience.

We'll start with "interest" audiences.

INTEREST AUDIENCES

Open up the Audiences tab inside your Meta Ads Manager.

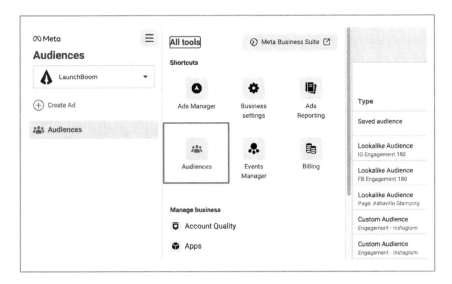

Click on the "Create Audience" button and then click on "Saved audience."

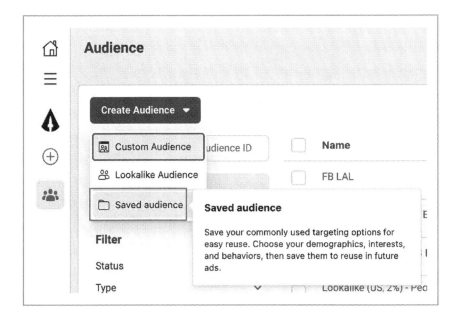

Enter all of the basic demographic information (age, gender, location, language). Here's an example:

Only target the countries that (1) you know you're going to ship your product to, and (2) speak the language in the ads. With that said, I recommend allocating the majority of your budget towards the US, as that's where the majority of Kickstarter and Indiegogo are.

Here's an example of age, gender, and language:

Next, look at your Dream 20, choose one of the brands you listed, and enter that brand into the Interests field. If your brand was Dollar Shave Club, it would look like this:

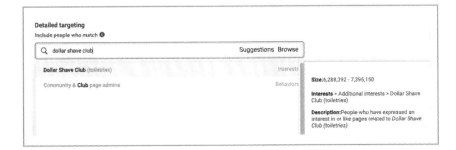

Then click on "Suggestions."

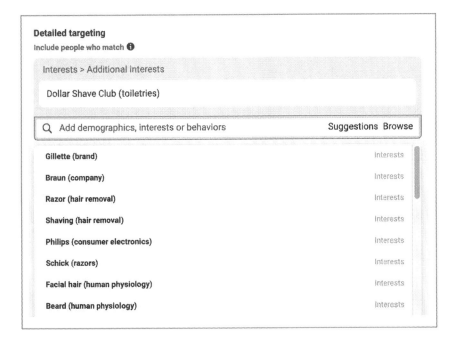

Next, Meta lists other interests that it deems relevant to the interest you entered. Meta is extremely good at suggesting interests.

To begin building your audience, start by choosing some of the Meta-suggested interests. I recommend selecting additional brand-based versus topic-based interests, if possible. Stop when the potential reach of your audience is somewhere between 12 and 15 million people.

Last, enter any exclusions or narrowing parameters. We call this "refining your audiences."

REFINING YOUR AUDIENCES

By following the methodology described so far to create your interest audiences, you are 90 percent there. You can supercharge your audience targeting by using "narrowing" and "exclusion" techniques. With narrowing, the audience becomes more targeted through the use of some clever options. With exclusions, some audience members who we know will not convert are removed.

I'll go over the basic options we use to refine most of our audiences.

Exclusions

- Custom audiences: Exclude all of your lookalike audiences, other lists, and web traffic custom audiences.
- Locations: Exclude locations where you don't want your ad to appear. For example, you should not be advertising a snow-related product in Hawaii.

Narrowing

- Demographics: Choose an age range and gender that you believe matches your target customer.
- Language: *Always* select English All under language, unless you plan to run ads in a different language.
- Technology: If your product requires a certain technology to operate, make sure you narrow by that technology. For example, if you're selling a product that only works with iPhones, narrow by iPhone users.
- Platform: Narrow by Kickstarter, Indiegogo, and Crowdfunding, because people who know about Kickstarter and Indiegogo are more likely to purchase. This is especially necessary if you're targeting internationally. I don't always use this one, but most of our top-performing audiences include this narrowing.

LOOKALIKE AUDIENCES

Meta is so powerful that it can build great audiences for you. All you need to do is give it a sample audience to base its targeting on. If you have a good seed audience, "lookalikes" will typically be the best-performing audiences.

To create your lookalike audience, go to the audiences section and click "Lookalike Audience" in the dropdown.

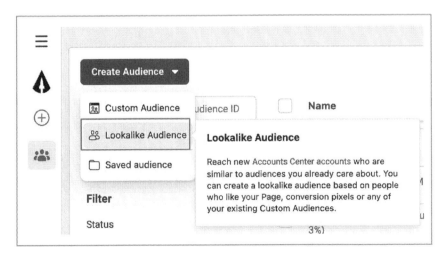

The best lookalike audiences are based on your customer lists. Even if you don't have an existing customer list, you can still generate a powerful lookalike audience.

Generate at least a thousand leads (the more the better) from your "interest" audiences. Create a lookalike audience of those people and target them. An audience that is based on leads (or better yet, on *reservations*) is going to be more qualified.

Creating Your Ad Imagery

You don't need to have professional imagery to create a successful ad for Meta. On the contrary, we've found that nonprofessional, authentic-looking imagery performs better.

On Facebook and Instagram, people are not looking to be sold to by a company. When they see an image that looks polished, they immediately think "ad." We don't want that thought to occur to them. Instead, use imagery that looks natural in their feed, yet still elicits enough curiosity for them to click.

Here are a few examples of what I mean.

IMAGERY EXAMPLE #1: TESTIMONIAL

With your phone, shoot a vertical video of someone using your product and giving a testimonial. So that it looks as natural and real as possible, do not edit the video.

The ad below is from our Xion eBike campaign, which raised $1,104,152 on Indiegogo. The ad imagery uses a video that I'm sorry I can't show you in this book – unfortunately that technology doesn't exist yet!

But this imagery worked so well that we ended up spending $48,337.04 just on this one ad in the prelaunch.

IMAGERY EXAMPLE #2: FOUNDER WALKTHROUGH

Another very popular ad type is what I call the "founder walkthrough" video, where the founder is filmed unpackaging the product and showing how it works. Like the previous ad, it's shot vertically on a phone, and there are no edits or cuts.

Here's an example from our campaign for the X300 projector that raised $239,098 on Indiegogo.

IMAGERY EXAMPLE #3: RED ARROW

Another very popular ad type is a static image that includes a tiny red arrow pointing to the product. Yes, that little red arrow actually works quite well. We've tested the exact same image, using one with the red arrow and one without the red arrow, and the red arrow always wins.

Here's an example from our campaign for Author Clock, which raised $2,217,773 on Kickstarter and Indiegogo InDemand.

WHAT'S THE COMMONALITY?

The examples I just presented are responsible for driving millions of dollars in revenue for those three campaigns. The common feature for all of them is that the ads were incredibly simple to make. We didn't spend thousands of dollars on high-end production. We actually shot two of them using a phone!

I recommend using Canva to create your ads — it's free! You can get a Canva account by scanning the QR code or going to crowdfunded-book.com/canva.

Writing Your Ad Copy

The two most important elements of your ad copy are (1) the top text section and (2) the bottom headline. You can see an example below from our campaign, TidyBoard, which raised $612,395 on Kickstarter.

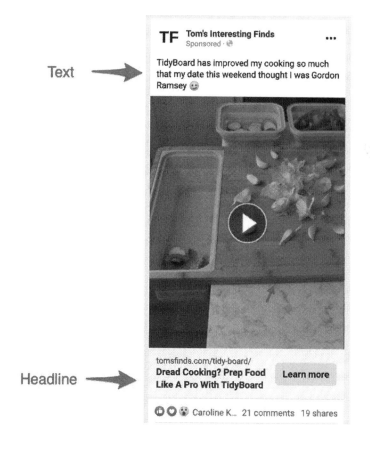

Most important is to keep your copy product-focused and not brand-focused.

I recommend stealing our best-performing ad templates by downloading the *LaunchBoom Ad Library*. Scan the QR code or go to <u>crowdfundedbook.com/ad-library</u>.

Program Your Ads

You just got a crash course in creating Meta ads. I know this is a lot of information, but you are now probably more knowledgeable about Meta ads than 95 percent of the world.

All you have to do now is take what you learned and program it into Meta's Ads Manager. *How will you do that*, you're wondering.

Well, I've got you covered there too, with a checklist you can use to make sure you program your ads correctly in Meta.

Download the *Meta Ad Checklist* by scanning the QR code or going to <u>crowdfundedbook.com/ad-checklist</u>.

Once everything is programmed, you'll start to see traffic flowing to your reservation funnel and your prelaunch email list beginning to grow.

And just like that, you've completed milestone #4!

CHAPTER

Advertising Metrics and Measuring Success

So, you've come up with your initial product positioning. You're ready to test multiple angles and audiences. You have your ad copy written. You have your ad images created. You've programmed everything into Meta and turned on your ads...

Now what?

There are hundreds of ad metrics that Facebook reports to you about: click-through rate, impressions, cost per lead...to name just a few. Which metrics should you be looking at to measure success?

Understanding the Model

Although each metric can give you some insight, there are two that will be the most important for your prelaunch: cost per reservation and cost per lead.

1. **Cost per reservation:** That's pretty self-explanatory. This is the average cost to get a reservation. How much it costs to get a reservation is something we'll track using what Meta calls "cost per purchase." In our case, this is a slight misnomer since visitors aren't exactly purchasing the product, but the deposit they leave qualifies them to be thought of in that way.

2. **Cost per lead:** Again, pretty self-explanatory. This is the average cost to get one lead or email.

At the end of the day, an ad is successful if it makes you money. Since you're in prelaunch, you can't directly track whether an ad will make you money or not. You can only make a prediction. These metrics allow you to make more accurate predictions.

To illustrate how this works, I've created a simple spreadsheet model you can refer to. Scan the QR code or go to <u>crowdfundedbook.com/</u> <u>ad-model</u> to download the *LaunchBoom Ad Model* and follow along.

Also, understand that models are built using past data to try to predict the future. Unfortunately, no model is perfect. They only steer you towards the truth. With that said, let's break down how this model works.

First, the leads you collect will be divided into two categories you're already familiar with:

1. **VIPs** are those who reserve by placing at least a $1 deposit.

2. **Non-VIPs** are those who provide their email addresses on your landing page, but don't put down a deposit.

Only a certain percentage of VIPs and non-VIPs will buy your product when you launch. That percentage is called the conversion rate. Because VIPs showed more purchase-intent by pulling out their credit card and putting down a deposit, it's safe to assume that VIPs will have a higher conversion rate than non-VIPs.

If you know how many leads you have (from both VIPs and non-VIPs) and the expected conversion rate for both segments, you can calculate your expected sales.

For example, let's say you have 100 VIPs and 900 non-VIPs. Your expected conversion rate for the VIPs is 30 percent. Your expected conversion rate for the non-VIPs is 1 percent. Using simple math we can calculate the expected number of sales.

- **VIPs:** 100 × 30% = 30 expected sales
- **Non-VIPs:** 900 × 1% = 9 expected sales

Now we're getting closer to calculating expected revenue. The last step is to multiply your expected sales by your expected average order value. Average order value is the total revenue divided by the total sales over a certain time period.

Here's how I calculate the expected average order value for the model. By looking over data from our past campaigns, I've found that the average order value hovers around 1.25x – 1.5x the lowest price point of the product. So you can take your most discounted price and multiply it by 1.25 to get your expected average order value. (I use 1.25 to be conservative with my estimates.)

Why are we using expected *average* order value, instead of the price of a single unit? Well, when you launch your campaign, there will be a portion of your leads who purchase more than one unit and/or who purchase add-ons. That will make your average order value higher than the price of a single unit.

You can work through this example with me to calculate your expected average order value.

Let's say your lowest price point is $450. Multiply that by 1.25 and you'll get $562.50 as your expected average order value.

Using the number of expected sales that we calculated above, and the expected average order value, you can calculate the expected total revenue.

- **VIPs:** 30 sales × $562.50 = $16,875.00 expected revenue
- **Non-VIPs:** 9 sales × $562.50 = $5,062.50 expected revenue

That would put your total expected revenue at $21,937.50 ($16,875.00 + $5,062.50).

The last step is to divide the total expected revenue (in this case, $21,937.50) by the amount you spent on advertising, which will give you the expected return on ad spend (ROAS).

For example, let's say you spent $5,000 on advertising. The equation would look like this:

$21,937.50 ÷ $5,000.00 = $4.39 (We round up to the nearest penny.)

This means that for every ad dollar you spent, you made $4.39. Not too shabby.

Using the Model to Measure Advertising Success

There are two areas in the spreadsheet model, "Scenario 1" and "Scenario 2." You can use these two different areas to calculate the expected ROAS of two advertisements. This will tell you which advertisement is more likely to make you money.

A REAL-LIFE EXAMPLE: eWHEELS V2

Let's look at data from the prelaunch advertising for our client, eWheels V2. We did a lot of testing for eWheels V2, which is part of the reason why we raised $233,699 in the first 24 hours of the campaign.

We're going to take a look at two different advertisements from the prelaunch, where the only variable was the imagery – the copy and the audiences were identical. Isolating one variable lets us more accurately measure how it affects the metrics.

Here are the two ads:

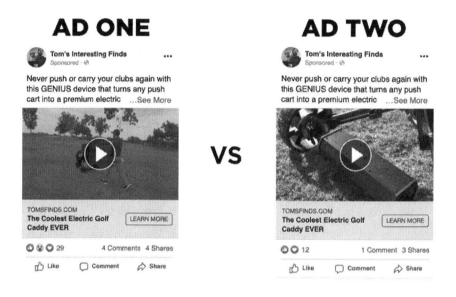

The ad spend for #1 was $112.99. It collected sixty leads, and thirteen of those put down a $1 deposit and became VIPs.

We spent $46.15 on ad #2, collected twenty-two leads, and one of those leads put down a $1 deposit to become a VIP.

Let's plug these numbers into the model. First, let's start with the *global variables*, which are the variables that equally apply to both ads:

Global Variables	
Launch Day Price	$450.00
Average Order Value	$562.50
Reservation Deposit	$1.00
VIP Conversion Rate	30%
Non-VIP Conversion Rate	1%

Next, let's put in the ad metrics to see our cost per lead and cost per reservation. Just as a reminder:

- Cost per lead = Ad spend ÷ number of leads
- Cost per reservation = Ad spend ÷ number of reservations (Reservations here equal number of VIP leads)

SCENARIO 1		SCENARIO 2	
Totals		*Totals*	
Ad Spend	$112.99	**Ad Spend**	$46.15
Total Leads	60	**Total Leads**	22
-- VIP Leads	13	*-- VIP Leads*	1
-- Non-VIP Leads	47	*-- Non-VIP Leads*	21
Cost / Lead	$1.88	**Cost / Lead**	$2.10
Cost / Reservation	$8.69	**Cost / Reservation**	$46.15

Lastly, let's see what our expected returns are. Using the data you find in the examples above in our eWheels V2 example, make the following calculations and you'll arrive at what shows in the chart below.

How to make the various calculations:

- Deposit revenue = Number of VIP leads (reservations) × $1
- VIP revenue = Number of VIP leads × VIP conversion rate × average order value
- Non-VIP revenue = Number of non-VIP leads × non-VIP conversion rate × average order value
- Total revenue = VIP revenue + non-VIP revenue + deposit revenue
- ROAS = Total revenue ÷ ad spend dollars
- ROAS percentage = Total revenue ÷ ad spend dollars × 100

SCENARIO 1		SCENARIO 2	
Expected Returns		*Expected Returns*	
Deposit Revenue	$13.00	**Deposit Revenue**	$1.00
VIP Revenue	$2,193.75	**VIP Revenue**	$168.75
Non-VIP Revenue	$264.38	**Non-VIP Revenue**	$118.13
Total Revenue	$2,471.13	**Total Revenue**	$287.88
Return On Ad Spend (ROAS)	2187.03%	**Return On Ad Spend (ROAS)**	623.78%

Based on this model, it's easy to see that ad #1 has a higher likelihood to drive revenue than ad #2 does. That is why we stopped testing ad #2, and continued to spend on ad #1.

Applying the Model to Your Ads

Now that you understand how the model works, you can apply it to your own advertising tests. Test copy that details different features of your product. Test imagery to see what captures attention. Test different audiences to see who really resonates with your product.

Take all the data you collect and plug it into the model to see which ad has a higher likelihood of driving more revenue. Continue to run the winning ad. Stop using the ad that lost. Create a new test. Rinse and repeat.

This is how you systematically test your positioning. When you launch, you'll be confident in your ability to convey the value of your product to the right audience. You'll have the data to back it up.

Furthermore, you will now have a prelaunch email list of people you know are qualified, backed up by your data. Meaning, you will have a list of people who want to buy your product! A list that will get you funded the first day!

How to Fix a Leaky Funnel

Imagine a funnel with water being poured into it. Now imagine that funnel with dozens of holes in it. Water leaks everywhere. This obviously needs fixing.

The same is true for your reservation funnel. But instead of losing water, you're losing visitors. You can identify these holes using math. And once you spot the problems, you can start to fix them.

There are three reasons that most product creators struggle to fix funnel leaks. They are missing some important information, so they:

- Don't track the right metrics
- Don't know if their metrics are good
- Don't know what to do if their metrics are bad

You're about to learn how you can easily overcome all of these problems. To start, let's zoom out to get an overview of the entire funnel.

How to Build a Watertight Reservation Funnel

As you already know, the reservation funnel builds a list of real buyers before you launch. But with multiple steps to this funnel, there are many chances for visitors to "leak" out of the funnel. There are also many different metrics that can be tracked.

This can be overwhelming, so let me clarify your goal, the most important metric to track, and the benchmark you should be shooting for.

OVERALL GOAL

Above all, the goal of the reservation funnel is to collect reservations. With that in mind, let's break down the primary goal metric.

Here's your goal: to collect reservations.

- **Key metric:** Cost per reservation (CPR)
- **Benchmark:** Not more than 25 percent of your product's price point (with a maximum of $50 CPR)

We want your CPR to be 25 percent of the price point of your product, at the max – except we never want the CPR to be over $50, no matter the price point.

That means if your product is $100, you want your CPR to be $25 or less. If your product is $1,000, you want your CPR to be $50 or less, because *we never want the CPR to be over $50.*

What does it mean if my CPR is higher than 25 percent of the price point of my product?

There's a leak in your funnel, which means somewhere in your funnel there is a need for optimization.

For the rest of this lesson, we're going to go deep into how to identify the leaks. More importantly, I'll teach you how to fix them.

Let's start with step one of your funnel: ads.

FUNNEL STEP #1: ADS

Ads, the first touchpoint someone has with your funnel, are the hook. Your goal is to grab someone's attention and make them click on your ad, starting them on the journey down your funnel.

Here's your goal: to have someone click on your ad.

- **Key metric:** Click-through rate (CTR)
- **Benchmark:** 3 percent CTR

We want at least 3 percent of people who see the ad to click on it.

An ad's performance is affected by two primary things: (1) the audience you are targeting, and (2) the ad creative. We've already talked about audience targeting, so I'm assuming that you're set there. Now we'll focus on the creative.

What does it mean if my CTR is below 3 percent?

That's an easy answer: You aren't grabbing people's attention quickly enough.

Your ad's creative is made up of these three parts, listed in order of impact (from highest to lowest):

1. Imagery
2. Copy
3. Headline

The example above is from our Lomi campaign, which raised $7,228,029 on Indiegogo, and you can see all the parts of the ad.

Imagery is the most important because it's where people's eyes go first when they spot your ad. Therefore, if you're at *below* 3 percent CTR, you should test your imagery first. Don't try to test multiple variables at once, because then you can't know which variable causes your CTR to change.

FUNNEL STEP #2: LANDING PAGE

Now that you've hooked an audience hungry for answers, you want to feed them. That's why I call your landing page the meat – it satiates curiosity's hunger by answering why your product will solve a particular problem.

Here's your goal: to collect an email address (lead).

- **Key metric:** Conversion rate (CR)
- **Benchmark:** 20 percent CR

We want at least 20 percent of all visitors to your landing page to become leads.

A landing page is filled with much more information than an ad. You have to answer the visitor's question "Why should I want this product?" So there are many more variables that have an impact on the conversion rate.

What does it mean if my CR is below 20 percent?

People don't think your product is going to solve their problem.

That's because you aren't explaining well enough why your product solves their problem. As you learned before, there are a few variables that will have a much larger impact on conversion rate than others (listed from highest to lowest, in order of impact):

1. Headline
2. Body text
3. Image

As with the imagery in your ads, people's eyes will go to your headline first. For this reason, we test this first. It's also a plus that headlines are much easier to test than imagery.

FUNNEL STEP #3: CHECKOUT

Every earlier step has required virtually no commitment from your potential customer, but now it's time to really call them to commit. At this step, you offer them the chance to reserve your VIP offer by putting down at least a $1 deposit. A monetary commitment (even of $1) is a much higher commitment than anything they've done so far.

Here's your goal: to collect reservations.

- **Key metric:** Lead-to-reservation rate (LTR)
- **Benchmark:** 4 percent LTR

We want at least 4 percent of all leads to put down a deposit to become a reservation.

This is the first time you'll release your product's retail price and the deal you will be offering.

What does it mean if my LTR is less than 4 percent?

People don't think the VIP offer is worth it.

This means the perceived value of your VIP offer isn't high enough to justify the deposit. In that case, the best variable to test at this step is your VIP offer. As part of that, you can test:

- Your price point
- A different exclusive add-on
- A greater discount percentage

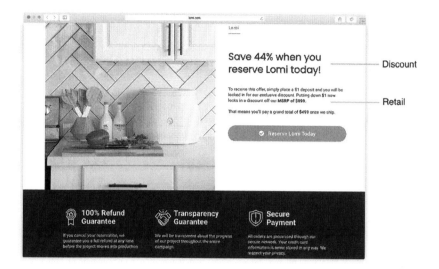

I see most clients either (1) increase the retail price or (2) maintain the retail price and increase the discount percentage. Both options end up increasing the discount, which makes the VIP offer more appealing.

Use This Framework to Improve Your Funnel

Hopefully your head isn't spinning too much from all the numbers! If it is, don't worry, it will all become clear as you start to apply the learnings. This chapter is a good one to flip back to once you start advertising and have your own real, earned data to consider.

The most important thing to remember is that your cost per reservation (CPR) matters the most! You don't want to go wild optimizing your funnel if your CPR is really good.

For example, let's say your CPR was 10 percent of your product's price point. That's 15 points lower than the benchmark, which is 25 percent, so you'd be looking really good. Even if your landing page was converting at 15 percent, I wouldn't recommend making major overhauls to it because your CPR is so good.

With that said, just know that most product creators don't hit the CPR benchmark right out of the gate. If that's you, the tips in this chapter will be extremely helpful, because little by little, you can fix the leaks and build a "watertight" reservation funnel.

CHAPTER

Adopting a Testing Mindset

At the beginning, LaunchBoom's business model was different than it is today. In 2015, if you and I had decided to work together, that meant our team and your team were committing to a collaboration for at least six months. That required a large investment of time and money from both parties, which meant a great deal of risk.

We saw a lot of success with our initial clients, but we also saw a campaign or two struggle early on. Trying to define some reasons, we found that, in a couple of cases:

- Building the prelaunch email list was much more expensive than planned.
- The original positioning of the product wasn't resonating.
- We were just beating our heads against a wall trying to make it work.

So yes, in some cases, we would launch and unfortunately…it didn't work.

Having experiences like that forced our team to ask some difficult questions — including the most important question of all: **How can we know if a campaign is going to be successful** *before* **we launch on Kickstarter or Indiegogo?**

We found an answer. **We test it.**

Instead of having clients invest a huge amount of time and money into their product launch, we thought... To ensure viability, why don't we drastically reduce the risk by testing the product in the market *before* we launch?

And of course, every day we hear the same questions from product creators:

- How do I raise $[insert any amount here] on Kickstarter or Indiegogo?
- How much do I have to spend on advertising?
- What will be my return on investment?

Whoever provides answers to these questions without testing your product first is lying to you.

Sure, someone can use their intuition and past experience to give you their *opinion*, but that opinion isn't using any data that's directly tied to *your* product. To answer those questions more accurately, you must spend time and money on advertising to test product positioning and audience targeting.

We call this system **TestBoom**.

Here's an overview of how the TestBoom system works:

1. Develop initial hypotheses of how your product should be positioned in the market.
2. Build a reservation funnel and drive traffic to test your hypotheses.
3. Analyze the data using a predictive model.

This testing system is incredibly important to learn and, luckily, it's something anyone can do.

Why Does This Matter So Much?

Even though launching through crowdfunding drastically reduces the risk versus other funding options, it still has its own risks. Everything does. Adopting a testing mindset and learning a testing system will decrease that risk even further.

People who are successful in business understand that it's a never-ending set of experiments. There will constantly be new business ideas you'll want to prove or disprove, which we can call hypotheses. These new business ideas will have to be tested, using what we can call experiments. These experiments will provide data to prove or disprove your hypotheses, as you conduct your analysis.

Ah yes, we're back in science class, but only for a minute. Just understand that using experimentation is key to not only your launch success, but to your business success.

A framework I love is called the "Build, Measure, Learn" loop, first created by Eric Ries in his book, *The Lean Startup*.

The framework is simple.

Build an experiment. Measure the data. Learn from the data.

This process will allow you to answer important questions about your product such as:

- Do people want to buy my product?
- How should I position my product?
- What will I have to spend on ads to achieve my goals?

Right now, you have a product that you *think* people want. But you do not *know* that people want it yet. It's pure hypothesis at this point.

It's very easy to get emotionally attached to your product. I get it – it's almost like your baby. But going into a launch believing that there is *no way* it's not going to be wildly successful is, to be blunt, a recipe for disaster.

I'm not saying you can't have big goals, but there's a giant difference between aiming for a big goal and believing there is *no way* you won't achieve it.

To put it another way: the testing mindset requires you to be open to being wrong.

Let me tell you the story of Heshika and his product, SPRYNG.

When we first started working with him, he told us that he thought his product would be best for athletes who needed a muscle recovery tool. We also knew the product would work for people who were more sedentary and had circulation problems. Essentially, the *opposite* audience in terms of physical fitness.

Neither Heshika nor the LaunchBoom team knew which positioning would be better. So we tested it and let the data decide.

We had half of our ads targeted towards athletes and the other half towards people with circulation problems.

Here's the copy that targeted athletes:

"Monster leg sessions in the gym, long days at the office, and marathon runs... Spryng is there for you, ready to aid your recovery and make you feel great, no matter what!"

Here's the copy that targeted people with circulation problems:

"Almost 90% of the blood returning to your heart from your veins comes from your calves. Exercise and long bouts of sitting/standing can weaken the muscles which makes them less effective in moving the blood, which can result in a lot of swelling and pain (known as blood pooling). This recovery tool focuses on actively compressing that area to help get that blood moving!"

The result…

The ads targeted towards those with circulation problems did *much* better. Because of that, we changed our positioning and started to spend more heavily into that audience.

By setting up an experiment to test our hypothesis, we gained extremely valuable information early in the prelaunch. That was all because Heshika had a testing mindset and followed our testing system. His campaign went on to raise $1,075,782 on Kickstarter and Indiegogo InDemand.

How This Works

We are going to take everything you've learned so far and create an experiment. To recap, you now know how to:

- Build your reservation funnel
- Drive traffic with Meta ads
- Track the right metrics

I suggest that you plan to spend $1,000 to $2,000 on ads for this initial experiment. Investing that much will likely give you enough data to answer some very important questions.

Here's a good illustration.

REAL EXAMPLE: AUTHOR CLOCK

Author Clock is an innovative clock that uses quotes from books to tell the time of day. The market hadn't seen a product like it before, so the testing period was especially important.

Over the course of two weeks, we created a reservation funnel, started driving traffic with Meta ads, and collected data.

At the end of our test, our metrics looked like this:

- Ad spend: $2,027
- Total VIPs: 173
- Total non-VIPs: 2,804

We put those metrics into our *TestBoom Predictive Model*, which you can download by scanning the QR code or going to <u>crowdfunded-book.com/testboom</u>.

The model works by taking the collected data and modeling three different scenarios. These three scenarios will give us a range of results from low to high conversion rates. But why three different scenarios?

That's because no models are 100 percent accurate. If they were, life would be a lot easier – we'd be able to predict the future. But giving a spread of future scenarios is still very useful because it provides a good idea of what's possible.

The first thing we did for Author Clock was plug in the data in the variables section of the model. You can see that below:

LAUNCHBOOM

Fill in your data below in the Variables section.
Anything that is highlighted can be changed.

VARIABLES

Ad Spend	$2,027
Total leads	2,977
# of VIPs	173
Launch day price	$99
Deposit amount	$1

It calculated three possible scenarios for the return on ad spend (ROAS) we could have expected if we were to launch right then. Here's that data:

ROAS (predicted)	Scenario	VIP Purchase Rate	Non-VIP Purchase Rate
3.34	Low	20%	0.67%
4.15	Normal	25%	0.83%
4.96	High	30%	1.00%

We also provide a nice graph so you can visualize the spread among the three scenarios.

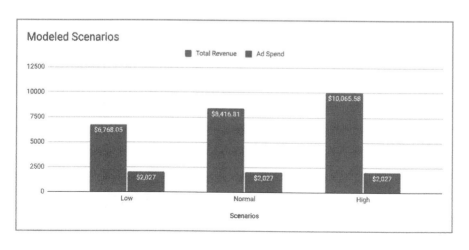

In the case of Author Clock, all three scenarios looked *very* good. So we felt confident that people wanted the product and we should move forward with the current positioning. Instead of going back to the drawing board with a major pivot in positioning, we decided to move into scaling the ads.

There Is No Wasted Ad Spend (when spent right)

If you're following the strategies I'm teaching in this book, there is simply no wasted ad spend. The dollars you might be afraid are "wasted" is actually money spent on education. This is a very important distinction.

If your initial test results aren't very good, it's easy to be discouraged and wonder "Why did I waste all this money on ads?" That'd be the wrong way to look at it.

Instead, you want to adopt a testing mindset and systematically learn from each additional experiment. By following this framework, you'll launch with an incredible amount of know-how, and most importantly, confidence.

CHAPTER

Advanced Reservation Funnel Tactics

Elon Musk.

All by themselves, those two words probably evoke strong emotions in you. He's become a very polarizing figure lately, but that's not what this is about. I ask you to forget about your love or hate for now… because I want to talk about an undeniably effective marketing and sales strategy he's used that you can, too.

Back in 2016, Elon Musk opened up reservations for the Tesla Model 3. People could put down a $1,000 refundable deposit to reserve it. The Model 3 wouldn't be delivered for at least 6 months. But by putting down a deposit now people could:

- Lock in the price
- Save their spot in line to receive their Model 3

If you put down a deposit, you would still have to pay the remaining amount at a later point. But given the benefits above, a lot of people put down deposits.

Musk's strategy performed extremely well. On the first day reservations were opened, Tesla took in over 200,000 deposits. After a few months, they had 450,000 deposits.

Let's do some quick math:

450,000 reservations × $1,000 deposit = $450,000,000 in revenue.

$450 million in revenue is mind-boggling. Remember, that revenue was only from *deposits*. Eventually each person would have to pay ~$45,000 more to complete their purchase... meaning the deposits only represented 2 percent of potential revenue.

Here's what the potential future revenue looked like:

450,000 reservations × $45,000 average price = $20,000,000,000 in potential revenue

Now, if you're thinking that not everyone completed their purchase, you'd be right. Many people did not complete their Model 3 purchase after the deposit, but it was still a huge success. Because of their strategy, Tesla was able to:

- Generate cash flow immediately
- Validate demand
- Predict future revenue

This is cool and is partly why Musk is one of the richest men in the world. But could it work for you?

Well, as I said earlier, this is not a strategy only for Elon Musk.

Taking Higher Deposits

As you know, the $1 deposit works.

It tells you which leads are more likely to convert so you can build a more qualified email list. The deposits also generate a little extra cash before you launch. However, after the payment processing fees, it's pretty close to nothing in the grand scheme of things.

Looking at how Tesla made $450,000,000 from deposits really got us thinking.

What if instead of taking $1, we took $50? Or maybe even $100? If we got a much larger amount of money in deposits, we could invest that into the prelaunch and scale our spend more aggressively, without needing our clients to cough up additional cash.

Our experimentation process started by looking for two things: price point and performance.

1. **Price point:** We needed a price point that was high enough to justify a higher reservation deposit. It makes sense to ask for a $50 deposit on a $500 product, but nobody would reasonably pay $50 to reserve a $75 product.
2. **Performance:** We needed to see a strong enough cost per reservation (CPR) on the $1 for it to make sense to try a higher reservation deposit. If we increased the price of the deposit, it's only natural that the CPR would increase as well. So, we needed a low-enough starting CPR to have room for that possible spike.

We decided to test this on two campaigns: Nomad's Pad and Xion CyberX.

- Nomad's Pad had a $500 price point, and was getting a CPR as low as $8.
- Xion CyberX was at a $2,900 price point, and was getting a CPR as low as $35.

For Nomad's Pad, we upped the $1 reservation to $50. For Xion, we upped it to $100.

The results were incredible.

Using Deposits to Subsidize Ad Spend (and even *earn* money!)

Not only did we generate leads that were way more likely to convert (up to eighty-five times more likely than a regular lead for Nomad's Pad), but we were also able to pump the deposits we were collecting back into our prelaunch to subsidize ad spend. This significantly reduced our actual cost per reservation and our client's out-of-pocket costs.

On Nomad's Pad, we actually went cash-positive on reservation deposits alone! We were generating $50 reservations for as little as $42 each. Meaning, we made $8 for every reservation we got.

On Xion CyberX, each $100 deposit we took in cost us around $120. That meant we were earning around 80 percent cash back on our ad spend. By pumping the $100 deposits back into our prelaunch, we were able to spend $103,665.71 on ads, while earning back $84,987.83 in deposits. That means the total out-of-pocket ad spend was only $18,677.88.

I like to visualize this "virtuous cycle" of higher deposits like this:

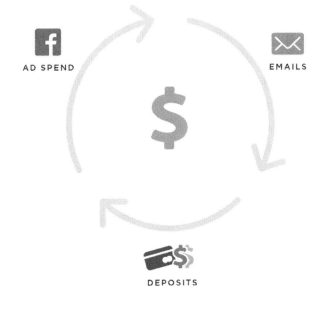

Here are the final, exact prelaunch performance numbers on both of these campaigns:

Nomad's Pad

- **Ad spend:** $44,515.80
- **Deposit revenue:** $45,803.79
- **Total prelaunch cost:** -$1,287.99 (Yes, that's negative. We actually went cash-positive and *made* over $1,200 during the prelaunch.)
- **$50 VIP conversion rate:** 22.34%
- **VIP revenue:** $358,602.00
- **Total prelaunch revenue:** $404,405.79
- **ROAS:** 9.1x

Xion CyberX

- **Ad spend:** $103,665.71
- **Deposit revenue:** $84,987.83
- **Total prelaunch cost:** $18,677.88
- **$100 VIP conversion rate:** 33.24%
- **VIP revenue:** $813,019.00
- **Total prelaunch revenue:** $898,006.83
- **ROAS:** 8.7x

What About Refunds?

You're probably wondering, "Do you really get to keep all those deposits? Nobody who didn't end up purchasing wanted their money back?"

Across all our campaigns, we've never seen a refund rate from VIP deposits higher than 2 percent. Even though the deposits are refundable, and we make sure to share that on our landing pages, most people just write off that deposit when they decide not to convert.

This Won't Work for Everyone

This is an advanced tactic, but as I said before, it will only work if your price point is high enough. If you are (1) seeing great results with the $1 deposit, and (2) have a price point that justifies an increase, go for it!

We increased pretty aggressively with Nomad's Pad and Xion CyberX, but you can start smaller with a $5 or $10 deposit to see how it performs. The $5 and $10 deposits can work with price points that are much lower. They likely aren't going to give you the same type of subsidized ad spend as in the examples I showed you, but they're much better than $1.

CHAPTER

Nurturing Your VIP Community

Your VIP community is an often-underrated asset. Once someone upgrades to VIP, it's best to give them the option to join an exclusive community of early adopters of your product. You have much to gain when they can communicate directly with you, your team, and other members of the community.

Earlier, I told you to be careful not to email your prelaunch list too much. Well, with the VIP groups, that advice doesn't apply. The VIP group requires faster and more frequent communication. And since it's a community forum, it's important that people are active and engaged, or no one will want to be a part of it. Nurturing community in this group is essential to your product launch.

Setting Up Your VIP Community

The two most common tools we use to set up VIP communities are Facebook groups and Discord servers.

FACEBOOK GROUPS

Facebook groups, which are free and easy to set up, are the ones we use the most. And because almost everyone has a Facebook account, they're very accessible.

I recommend making your Facebook group private so that people have to request to join, making it feel much more exclusive. Here's a Facebook group we set up for our campaign, SPRYNG, which raised $1,075,782 on Kickstarter and Indiegogo InDemand.

DISCORD

Discord servers are particularly popular in the gaming category. If your products falls into that category, you should probably use Discord. Discord servers are free to set up as well, but have some advanced features you can pay for if you want some customization.

One of the coolest parts about Discord is that you can organize your VIP community by different topics. Here's a screenshot from the VIP Discord server for Alpha Clash:

On the left side, you can see how users can gravitate towards different topics. This keeps conversations more organized than in Facebook groups.

How to Engage

Keeping your VIP group engaged is essential. Ideally, you'll get to a place where your VIP members are posting too, but you shouldn't expect that at the beginning. First, you have to give them something to talk about.

Here are topics that I recommend starting with:

WELCOME NEW MEMBERS

When new members come in, give them a warm welcome. Tag them in a post and show them some love. It's a super-easy way to show new members you care that they decided to become a part of your community. Here's an example from etee:

SHARE UPDATES AND SEEK FEEDBACK

There's a lot going on leading up to your launch. Share that progress with your VIP community. You can let them have a taste by posting:

- A rough draft of your campaign video
- A draft of your campaign page
- Product-related updates

Ask for feedback to make the experience of launching feel more collaborative. These early adopters are the ones who are most passionate about your product. Their feedback can be extremely valuable, and making them feel connected is also extremely valuable.

ANNOUNCEMENTS

Big announcements should always be shared with the community, the most important being the planned launch date (and time). Here's an example of us sharing that announcement for SPRYNG.

By this point, you may be wondering "What in the world is Tom's Interesting Finds?" It's a product discovery brand we own that we use to share new, interesting products.

CELEBRATIONS

As you hit certain milestones, share the good news with the community! For our EcoTrek Adventure Pants campaign that raised $514,624 on Kickstarter, every time we got another hundred VIPs in the group, the founder made an announcement.

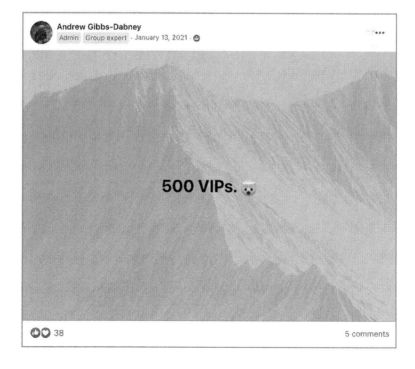

PRODUCT EDUCATION

Share details about what makes your product so great. It will have multiple benefits and features, so break each one out and write a post about it. We have a good example from Alpha Clash, where the founder created a YouTube video going through the game mechanics.

PROMOTION

This one's easy – remember to promote your launch when you go live! Share updates about the launch, including how much you've raised, how many backers you have, and other notes about your overall campaign success.

This Is a Long-Term Asset

If you do this right, your VIP group won't fade away after the launch. Continue to engage and build the group. Many of our clients ultimately invite all of their customers to join and treat it like a special place where everyone can interact.

My favorite example of a client who's turned a VIP group into a business asset is etee. They created a group back in 2019 for their Indiegogo launch, and they never stopped engaging. Now there are almost 4,000 VIP members and they're *super*-engaged – and useful, too.

etee asks their VIPs for product feedback. They get beta testers for new products. They promote sales… and much more.

You can do this too.

This is your opportunity to begin building a VIP group that will support your launch, and will also support the long-term success of your business. If you do it right now, you'll be able to benefit for many years to come.

CHAPTER

30-Day Reservation Funnel Challenge

W e just went over *a lot*. If you're feeling a little overwhelmed, just take a breath. You can do this, by just going step-by-step. And now you have a blueprint to help you start building your prelaunch email list.

It bears repeating – this is the *most* important part of the whole process.

Which is why I want to make sure you actually get it done :)

Everyone's worked on big projects before, whether it was a college paper, remodeling a house, or an important presentation. Whatever it was, we all know the feeling of starting at zero and dreading all the steps it will take to get to the end.

If you're concerned about being swamped with all the steps as you build your reservation funnel, I have good news for you. You are *not* starting from scratch.

In this chapter, I'll show you how you can use our software and templates to build your reservation funnel *and* get ads live…in as little as thirty days.

And I am here to tell you that once you press the "ads live" button, it will really start to feel real. You'll have the momentum you need to launch – and bring your product idea to life.

Setting Up Your Reservation Funnel

I'm going to walk you through the four major steps of getting your reservation funnel created and your Meta ads live.

STEP 1: WRITE YOUR LANDING PAGE CONTENT

Before you start developing your reservation funnel, take time to write out all the content you plan to use. I suggest downloading our *Landing Page Content Template*, and also look at examples of landing pages we've built. Scan the QR code or go to crowdfundedbook.com/landing-page.

Then all you have to do is fill in the template and you'll have the first draft of your landing page content.

Action items:

- Download our *Landing Page Content Template*.
- Review examples of best-performing landing pages.
- Write the draft of your own landing page content.

STEP 2: BUILD YOUR RESERVATION FUNNEL

With the content written, you're ready to start building your reservation funnel. This gets a little more technical. But don't worry, I have you covered here too.

There are a few pieces of software that make it easy to set up. I recommend checking out ClickFunnels, Leadpages, or LaunchKit.

LaunchKit was created by my team at LaunchBoom and is the technology that powers all of our launches.

Scan the QR code or go to crowdfundedbook.com/launchkit to learn more.

Action items:

- Choose a funnel building software.
- Build your reservation funnel!

STEP 3: SET UP EMAIL MARKETING

After you've built your reservation funnel, you'll need a place to store all your contacts so you can market to them for your crowdfunding launch. Currently (as I write this, in the first half of 2023), I recommend Mailchimp. It's super-easy to set up and works really well with LaunchKit.

Scan the QR code or go to crowdfundedbook.com/mailchimp to sign up for your account.

I recommend upgrading to the paid plan they have so you can use the features we use for our email marketing campaigns.

Action items:

- Sign up for your Mailchimp account.
- Download our *Welcome Emails Template*: crowdfundedbook.com/email.
- Write the welcome emails.
- Program those welcome emails into Mailchimp.

STEP 4: PROGRAM YOUR META ADS

The last step is to get your Meta ads programmed. Re-read the chapter "Driving Traffic With Paid Ads" to learn the fundamentals. Then go through the steps below.

Action items:

- Sign up for a Meta Business Account: business.facebook.com.
- Program your initial audiences using your Dream 20.
- Create your ad copy and imagery using our *LaunchBoom Ad Library*: crowdfundedbook.com/ad-library.
- Program your initial ads into Meta. You can download a free ad training video by scanning the QR code or going to crowdfundedbook.com/ad-training.

Planning Your Project

Completing this challenge in thirty days is very possible. And it's much easier if you employ some basic project management. I recommend following these simple best practices:

DETERMINE YOUR END GOAL

Choose a date by which you'll have this completed. The idea may sound obvious, but many people *don't* do this and it ends up taking them months to get their reservation funnel up.

Open your calendar. Choose the date. Done!

DEFINE YOUR TIMELINE

Above, I provided the steps that must be taken to complete this thirty-day challenge. Assign completion dates to each of the individual steps.

Don't overthink this. Pull up Google Docs or a notepad and put your best estimation of when each task will be done, in writing, so you can hold yourself accountable.

PUT IT IN YOUR CALENDAR

Now that you have dates for every task, put them in your calendar! Or if that's not your thing, use some project management software like Asana (which is free, and if you're looking for something like that, it's good to know).

Use whatever is your favorite way to manage a project. The most important thing is that your project is planned and due dates assigned.

Three Keys to Completing This Challenge

USE OUR SOFTWARE

I know I seem to be plugging my software a lot, but that's because I know it will save you *so* much time and money if you use it. It's purpose-built to create reservation funnels and includes all the analytics and tech we've been building and refining since 2015.

This will be the easiest way to fast-track your progress.

Learn more at crowdfundedbook.com/launchkit.

DONE IS BETTER THAN PERFECT

As a perfectionist myself, I understand wanting everything to be 100 percent before I let it go live. But with respect to this example of "Do what I say, not what I may have done once" – that's not the way you should think about this. It's easy to get stuck on tiny details to the point that it's just an excuse to continue delaying having your funnel go live.

You can always go back and improve your funnel later. Focus on getting it done, not making it perfect.

ACCOUNTABILITY

Product creators and entrepreneurs can travel a lonely path, sometimes. And everyone doesn't always have a "someone" to push and hold them accountable. Well, it doesn't have to be that way.

Once you bought this book, you became eligible to join a community of hundreds of other product creators like you – along with me and my team. There's no additional charge to sign up since you bought this book.

Join us at crowdfundedbook.com/community.

Lean on the community when you need support, motivation, or even (or, especially!) to celebrate your progress! You don't have to go at this alone.

Complete This Challenge and You Won't Be Stopped

This is true: If you complete the 30-Day Reservation Funnel Challenge, you'll have so much momentum that your launch will be inevitable. There's something so powerful about getting your ads live and watching your first leads come through. Without a doubt, you've found people who are interested in buying your product!

You are only thirty days away from experiencing that feeling – if you really want to. I hope you accept the challenge. And thirty days from now, I hope to see you celebrating your accomplishment with the *LaunchBoom Community.*

PART 4:
GETTING READY TO LAUNCH

Designing Your Campaign Page

Your campaign page is one of your most important marketing assets. This is the page everyone will see when you launch, so the design of this page absolutely must be top-notch.

A great campaign page design is more than just pretty pictures. It's a mix of persuasive copywriting, eye-catching visuals, and storytelling.

Since you've already put so much work into testing your product positioning during the prelaunch, creating the content will be easier for you than it would have been otherwise.

The process of designing your campaign page can be broken down into two parts: (1) writing persuasive copy, and (2) creating the visuals. Let's start with the first.

Writing Persuasive Copy

The copy has to come first. Once finalized, it's given to a designer (who may be you) to finish the visual aesthetics of the campaign page, somewhat based on the message and tone of your copy.

While most people will be able to write fairly good copy using what I'm about to teach you, great copywriting is a very sought-after skill that not many people have. If you know your copywriting skills are lacking, I recommend finding someone to support you here.

MODELING WHAT WORKS

Before you get started on writing your campaign page copy, I recommend researching successful campaigns similar to yours on Kickstarter. Get a feel for how your competitors are organizing their content, speaking to the consumer, and designing their pages. This will give you a comparative starting point for writing your copy.

Don't fall into the trap of thinking you have to reinvent the wheel. Keep it simple and model what works!

CAMPAIGN PAGE OUTLINE

The structure I'm about to review is from our *Campaign Page Template*. Download it and refer to it when writing your campaign page. Scan the QR code or go to crowdfundedbook.com/campaign-page.

I'm not going to talk about every section of the campaign page. Instead, I'm going to give you a few examples of how our resource works, and some tips on getting your campaign page done.

I'm also only going to be giving examples from Kickstarter. (There are some slight differences in character count and sizing on Indiegogo, but they're pretty close.)

OPENING SECTION

The opening section has three main elements:

1. Project name
2. Project description
3. Project image

Here's how it looks in the *Campaign Page Template* resource:

LAUNCHBOOM

CAMPAIGN PAGE TEMPLATE

Go to FILE and make a copy in your Google Drive or Download to your computer

Project Name (Kickstarter 60 characters max / Indiegogo 50 characters max):
Product Name - What is it?/What does it do? + What makes it different?
Or use your winning landing page hero headline - shortened to fit.

Product Description (Kickstarter 135 characters max / Indiegogo 100 characters max):
What value does it give?/What is it? + How does it do it?
Or use your winning landing page hero description - shortened to fit.

Project Image:
Use your top performing hero image or ad image. Can add graphics to it.
Needs to show the whole product.

Image link - 1920x1080 px for KS; 695x460 px for IGG
You can also use our drag and drop Canva templates

Here's an example of the template, completed with copy from our campaign for Author Clock:

LAUNCHBOOM
Campaign Page Content

Project Name (KS 60): Author Clock: A Novel Way To Tell Time

Project Description (KS 135): The first clock that displays the time through unique literary quotes *every* minute—this is time-telling reimagined.

Project Image:
Image of clock with iconic quote (ideally a minute-specific quote)

And then here's what it looks like on the Kickstarter page:

Obviously, the first thing people will see is the most important part. Luckily, it's not too difficult to get it right since you've been following the LaunchBoom system :)

I recommend using the best-performing headline and subheadline from your reservation funnel. These typically help in creating perfect project names and descriptions, since you have data to back up their effectiveness.

This same tactic can be used for your graphics. Find the best-performing image in your ads and use that as your all-important project image.

For Author Clock, following this process saved us a lot of time, and the campaign performed extremely well.

BE CLEAR, NOT CLEVER

Good copywriting prioritizes clarity over cleverness. No one is going to buy your product if they are at all confused about what you're trying to say. This isn't art, so you can't be fuzzy or impressionistic. You're looking for people to part with their hard-earned money.

Start with the headlines and subheadlines when you're writing your campaign page copy. Don't try to fill in the supporting text yet. The goal is for readers to understand all the most important parts of your product, just by taking in the headlines.

This is important, because before you have their complete attention, people are going to skim your page first.

Here's an example of headlines we wrote for Author Clock.

—

Author Clock: A Novel Way To Tell Time

A new quote every minute

Be part of the story

One for your wall, and one for your desk

Quality components that make a statement

Easy-to-read display

Long battery life means no clunky cables

—

Just by scanning the headlines, readers get a good idea of the main benefits of Author Clock. This is the type of clarity you want to have in your copywriting.

THE REMAINING SECTIONS

The rest of the Campaign Page Template resource breaks down every section that we recommend for your page. Just as with the opening section, you should be able to borrow copy from your reservation funnel and apply it here.

Once you've finalized the copy, it's time to move into design.

Creating the Visuals

Both Kickstarter and Indiegogo have built-in page editors. However, you'll have to create your visuals outside of the platforms. When that's done, you can use the built-in page editors to put all the pieces together and build your campaign page.

Unless you have professional design chops, again, I recommend using Canva. It's free and super-powerful. You can sign up here: crowdfundedbook.com/canva.

In the Campaign Page Template, we also link to Canva templates we made for you. (Another free resource that will speed up the process!)

DESIGN TIPS

This isn't going to be a master class in design, but I do have some tips that will be super-useful in designing your campaign page.

Use Feature Clouds

It's very common to show all the core features in a graphic I call a "feature cloud." Here's an example.

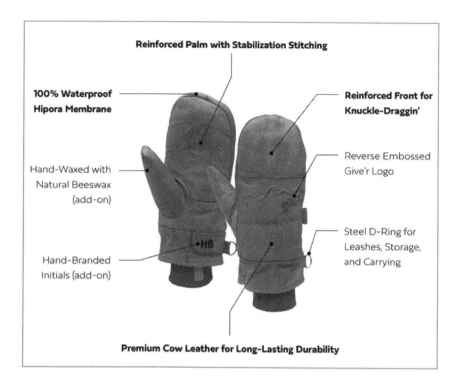

Use GIFs

GIFs are a great way to show your product in action and they come in handy when a still image just won't do. We often create GIFs from the campaign video to showcase key features.

Make Your Headlines and Subheadlines Images and Keep Supporting Copy as Text

We typically make our headlines and subheadlines as images that we upload to the page. We also keep this design style consistent throughout the page to build a visual hierarchy.

Here's an example of a headline style we kept consistent through the page:

GIVE'R TESTED: FROM THE EVERYDAY TO THE EXTREMES

Here's an example of the subheadline style we kept consistent through the page:

THE BEST FITTING MITTENS & WHY IT'S IMPORTANT

Also, all of your supporting copy should be written as text within the Indiegogo and Kickstarter page editors.

Bold and Italicize Text You Want to Emphasize

Use the Indiegogo and Kickstarter page editors to bold and italicize important text. Here's an example of supporting text where we did this.

The Frontier Mittens also keep your fingers together so they can share body warmth. This allows the inside of the mitten to work a bit like a furnace. Your fingers and hands circulate heat to each other while the mittens keep it all in, letting your body *retain its optimal functional temperature* with less effort.

Another Milestone Down!

I want to reiterate that it's important to *not* reinvent the wheel here. I understand wanting to add your own style, but don't be afraid to take advantage of what has been proven to work.

Research other successful projects on Kickstarter. Use the templates and examples I'm providing. Use the best-performing copy from your reservation funnel. Do these things and it's highly likely you'll make a great campaign page.

Just like that, you will have completed another milestone!

Creating Your Campaign Video

Ah, the campaign video. If I'm being honest, I have a bit of a love-hate relationship with it. On the one hand, it's an important asset that can have a big impact on your campaign, if done right. On the other hand, people can become obsessed with it, spending way too much time and money, and sometimes, even delaying their launch because of it.

Let's not have you fall into the latter category.

The campaign video, while important, is easy to spend *way* too much money on. If you get someone to do it for you, there's rarely a reason why you should spend more than $15K on it. And that's the high end.

In most cases, you should be able to get it created for *much* less than that.

Next, I'm going to show you what it takes to create a high-converting campaign video. You can then choose to do it yourself, hire an agency, or something in-between. Whatever you choose, the following information will be super-valuable.

Writing the Script

It all starts with a good script. As you probably guessed, I have a template for you.

You can download it here: crowdfundedbook.com/video.

I'm going to teach you how we write campaign video scripts by considering one from our campaign for BusyBox, which raised $332,202 on Indiegogo.

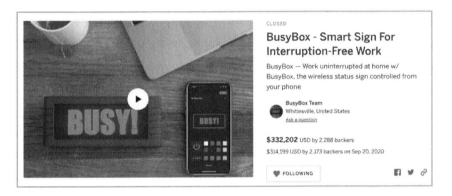

HOOK

The hook is all about grabbing a viewer's attention. The easiest way is to state the problem or the pain point your market is experiencing, through either a question or statement. Here's how we did it for BusyBox:

Rolls up chair

Turns on computer

Gets ready to work

Roommate BUSTS in

"HEY MAN! YOU BUSY?"

Leans back, sighs, and swivels in his gaming chair in frustration

Yes.

You are busy.

And it's time you let your house know it.

INTRODUCE THE PRODUCT

Now that you've hooked them with the problem, it's time to present your product as the solution.

Meet BusyBox.

The wireless status box that helps you work uninterrupted and enter deep focus at home.

HOW IT WORKS

Clearly and simply explain how it works.

BusyBox comes in two forms: Standard and Digital.

BusyBox Standard lets you slide in a choice of 6 messages to tell everyone in the house not to bother you.

BusyBox Digital lets you create and display your own custom messages or images to say "Leave me alone" however you want.

HOW TO SET IT UP

Clearly and simply explain how to set it up.

It's easy.

Mount the base to your door.

Choose or create your message.

Turn it on.

And get to work!

KEY FEATURES / BENEFITS

Go through each of the main benefits and supporting features of your product.

BusyBox will let everyone in the house know you're busy, so you can keep working without interruption.

Use the app to wirelessly turn BusyBox on and off. Or use the manual button if your phone is occupied.

You can even use Siri or Google Assistant for a complete touch-free experience.

Or sync with apps like Google Calendar to fully automate BusyBox to your schedule.

The app lets you choose colors and lighting modes to match your aesthetic and grab attention.

If you have multiple BusyBoxes, the app also allows you to group and control them all at once.

Customizable covers let you further personalize your BusyBox to match your style.

The battery is long lasting and quick to recharge — keeping your door wire-free.

USE HELPFUL INSTANCES

Explicitly state the places your customer would use your product.

Whether you're working remotely, video conferencing, streaming, recording, studying, editing, gaming, meditating, or even journaling, BusyBox will make sure your time and space stay interruption-free.

CLOSING SUMMARY

Reiterate the problem and the solution.

Staying focused and productive at home can be a challenge.

With BusyBox, it doesn't have to be.

CALL TO ACTION (CTA)

Tell them to buy your product!

Back our campaign today. And reclaim your focus with BusyBox.

Shooting and Editing the Video

If you want to shoot the video yourself, you don't need professional equipment that will burn a hole in your wallet and max out your credit card. You'd be impressed to see what you can do with an iPhone.

You might not be able to get the exact same look, feel, and control as with a high-end camera, but you can still make an extremely effective video.

Fun fact: we actually shot the entire video for ShiftCam (which raised $224,541) on an iPhone, and it helped us show the power of the product.

Here are some tips to making a video with an iPhone:

- Shoot videos horizontally if at all possible
- Don't zoom in (zooming decreases the quality)
- Edit the completed footage on your computer
- Use a tripod/stabilization (unless you're going for a *Blair Witch Project* vibe... and if you are...don't!). Feelings of nausea won't help your case.
- Use a good microphone: audio is *very* important

Or you can hire a professional, which is my preference.

Hire a Professional

Getting the video shot and edited to a high standard requires enough technical know-how that doing it all yourself is often out of the question. But there are a few ways you can bring costs of outsourcing down.

WRITE THE SCRIPT

Use the campaign script templates I've just shown you to write your initial script. Bringing your finished script to a video agency will save a lot of time and dollars. It's likely they will want to give you some feedback on it, which is great, but you can probably negotiate lower rates because you have that part done.

LIMIT TO ONE LOCATION

Tell the video agency that you only want to do a one-location shoot. The script you write will have to support this, meaning you can't have a script that has you at a lake, then in the snow, then at the beach... and expect the video production to be cheap.

SHOOT IT ALL IN ONE DAY

Be clear that you want to get the whole video shot in one day. This is very doable, especially if the script is relatively short. If you get pushback, ask the vendor what it would take to have it all shot in one day.

USE A LAUNCHBOOM EXPERT

Since we've been doing this for so long, we've worked with many video agencies. Some were bad (we're sorry to say), and some were great. We further vetted the great ones and added them to our LaunchBoom Expert network, indicating that we stand by their work. (Also, good for you to know: LaunchBoom clients get a discount from them!)

Get Your Campaign Video Made

You are now armed with the tools you need to create an amazing campaign video. Creating a video takes a lot of work, but it's also a lot of fun. And you get to flex your creative muscle.

And just like that, you will have completed another milestone!

CHAPTER

Choosing Between Kickstarter and Indiegogo

Here's one of the most frequently asked questions I've gotten since starting LaunchBoom:

Should I launch my crowdfunding campaign on Kickstarter or Indiegogo?

The answer is everyone's least favorite: *It depends.*

Each platform has its own strengths and weaknesses and there are multiple factors that will play into your final decision. If you review my past blog articles, you'll catch a glimpse of my struggling with this question, as I continued to learn more about what kinds of projects are best on each platform. In the next few pages, I'm aiming to provide you a detailed understanding of each platform as I know it now, so you'll know which one you should launch on.

Kickstarter

If I were to walk up to a random person on the street and ask them to name a crowdfunding platform, I'd put all my money on them saying "Kickstarter." That's because Kickstarter has simply done a better job of marketing their brand as synonymous with crowdfunding.

Even though they started after Indiegogo, Kickstarter has surpassed them in terms of funds raised and daily traffic. As of February 24, 2023, they had raised $7,123,991,477 from 583,964 projects and 21,778,166 backers. And of those 21 million backers, 7,453,068 have backed multiple projects.

According to SimilarWeb, a traffic estimator, Kickstarter sees an average of over 20 million unique visitors a month.

Of all the categories they support in this very impressive ecosystem they've built, it's useful to note that the top three categories in terms of total funding dollars are:

1. Games: $2.12 billion
2. Design: $1.54 billion
3. Technology: $1.33 billion

These stats usually surprise people, especially when they learn that the highest-earning category is games.

I'll tell you right now that if you have a game, you can skip the rest of this chapter and launch on Kickstarter. The community for games on Kickstarter is far bigger than on Indiegogo.

If you don't have a game, read on!

Indiegogo

Indiegogo broke into the crowdfunding scene before Kickstarter did. Initially it focused exclusively on independent films, which is where it got its name. It didn't take long for Indiegogo to start adding more categories.

This willingness to try new things is characteristic of Indiegogo's platform. Historically, they've simply been open to adding more features. They also have more flexible rules concerning the types of projects that can launch.

There's one thing they are not open about, though – their stats. Kickstarter has a page dedicated to live updating stats, but it's harder to gather Indiegogo's data. Through our research, we've been able to gather some metrics about them, in part by using traffic estimator websites like SimilarWeb.

The most recent public data I located was from an April 11, 2018 *Fast Company* article, in which Indiegogo stated that they'd raised close to $1.5 billion on their platform. Using the average amount raised per year since its founding, would mean they've probably raised close to $3B.

According to SimilarWeb, Indiegogo sees an average of about 7 million unique visitors a month.

Using these estimates, it looks like Indiegogo is about half the size of Kickstarter in terms of traffic and dollars raised. But that doesn't mean that Indiegogo is only 50 percent as effective as Kickstarter. There is much more that should be considered when assessing whether to use Indiegogo versus Kickstarter. We'll get to that in a moment.

Platform Differences

There are *a lot* of Kickstarter and Indiegogo features to compare. This format (the book you're reading right now) can't be up-to-the-minute on brand-new features, the way a website can be. But you can rely on the resources on our website, which we make sure to keep updated with the differences.

You can access that by scanning the QR code or going to <u>crowdfund-</u><u>edbook.com/ks-igg</u>.

The Crowdfunding Shakeup

Before I give you a framework for deciding which platform is best for your launch, I have to mention one thing.

In the last year or so, there have been some significant changes in the crowdfunding industry. I've watched BackerKit launch a crowdfunding platform to compete with Kickstarter. I've watched some of our competitors go out of business or shift focus. Perhaps the most consequential changes are with top leadership, as both Kickstarter and Indiegogo brought in new CEOs.

Indiegogo brought in their new CEO, Becky Center, in March of 2022. Before Indiegogo, she'd worked her way up through Groupon and then HealthJoy.

Kickstarter answered by bringing in their new CEO, Everette Taylor, in September of 2022. Prior to Kickstarter, he'd been the CMO of Artsy.

I've had great conversations with both of them. They each bring fresh perspectives and renewed energy to an industry that, admittedly, was somewhat stagnant.

One of the biggest changes since then has been on Kickstarter's end. Within a few months of assuming leadership, Everette announced that Kickstarter had added the Meta (Facebook) Pixel – something that we'd been pushing for, for nearly a decade.

The Meta Pixel used to be a huge advantage that Indiegogo had over Kickstarter. But that's no longer the case. From a marketing tools perspective, this levels the playing field between the two platforms.

It's also a sign that Kickstarter, with Everette's leadership, is looking to innovate, and quickly.

4-Step Decision-Making Framework

Basically, there are four questions that the decision framework rests on, and your decision may become obvious to you quickly.

Let's dive in!

STEP 1: WHAT COUNTRY DO YOU LIVE IN?

This one's easy. Not every country can launch on Kickstarter and Indiegogo. Here's the list (but be sure to check crowdfundedbook. com/ks-igg to get the most recently updated list):

Indiegogo – 33 countries

Australia, Austria, Belgium, Canada, Cyprus, Denmark, Estonia, Finland, France, Germany, Greece, Hong Kong, Ireland, Italy, Japan, Latvia, Lithuania, Luxembourg, Malta, Mexico, Netherlands, New Zealand, Norway, Poland, Portugal, Singapore, Slovakia, Slovenia, Spain, Sweden, Switzerland, the United Kingdom, and the United States.

Kickstarter – 25 countries

Australia, Austria, Belgium, Canada, Denmark, France, Germany, Greece, Hong Kong, Ireland, Italy, Japan, Luxembourg, Mexico, the Netherlands, New Zealand, Norway, Poland, Singapore, Slovenia, Spain, Sweden, Switzerland, the United Kingdom, and the United States.

Decision-making time

If your country isn't on this list, you may still be able to launch by using Stripe Atlas, which would allow you to create an entity in the US and open a US bank account from anywhere in the world.

If you're from one of the eight countries that Indiegogo supports and Kickstarter doesn't, you'll have to launch with Indiegogo.

If you're from one of the twenty-five countries they both share, read on for more decision points.

STEP 2: WHAT STAGE IS YOUR PROTOTYPE AT?

One of the biggest differences between the platforms is with rules around prototypes. On Kickstarter, you must have a functional prototype in order to launch. Their team will review your campaign page before you launch to make sure you clearly show that your product is capable of doing what you claim. This also means you are not permitted to use any photorealistic renderings on the page.

Indiegogo is different.

You can launch in what's called the "concept" stage, without having a functional prototype. That doesn't mean anyone can just launch a fraud. Indiegogo's Trust and Safety team reviews every project after they launch. They'll actually withhold funds from the creator until they are certain the product can be delivered. They'll even go as far as requesting signed documents from your manufacturer asserting that they are able to make your product.

In my opinion, Kickstarter's decision to require functional prototypes is better for the industry. It protects both the product creator and the backer. If the product creator has to come up with a functional prototype first, they are actually finding out what's possible, and so they are much less likely to make claims they can't back up. The backer is less likely to support something that might fall through, and they won't fall victim to scams.

Decision-making time

If you can't launch with a functional prototype for some reason, you'll have to choose Indiegogo.

If the decision hasn't been made for you yet, keep reading.

STEP 3: WHAT'S YOUR PRODUCT CATEGORY?

While both platforms are capable of launching nearly all the same product categories, certain of them perform better on a specific platform.

One explanation is that when a large campaign launches, other creators in the same category see that success and are more likely to launch on the same platform. Over a long-enough time horizon, enough projects from the same category launch on the same platform that a community of backers forms there as well. That community of backers makes launching on the platform even more effective.

Below you can see which specific product categories I'd recommend for each platform.

Kickstarter

1. Gaming (tabletop, trading card, etc.)

As I've said, if you have something in the gaming category, Kickstarter is your platform. Here's an example from our Pericle campaign.

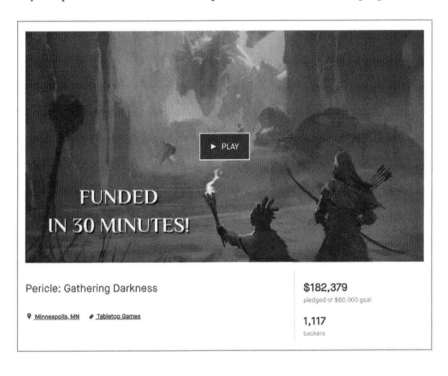

Pericle: Gathering Darkness

📍 Minneapolis, MN   🏷 Tabletop Games

$182,379
pledged of $60,000 goal

1,117
backers

2. Graphic novels / books

Graphic novels and books perform better on Kickstarter as well. Here's an example from our campaign for A Gay Man.

A Gay Man - The Illustrated Storybook Gay Men
Deserve

AU$ 66,940
pledged of AU$ 5,000 goal

521
backers

● Project We Love   ♥ Melbourne, AU   ✎ Fiction

3. Art / music / film

Art, music, film... these creative categories are no-brainers for Kickstarter.

Indiegogo

1. Lodging / glamping / hotels

This is an interesting category that will work only on Indiegogo. That's because you'll need to use photorealistic renderings on your campaign page and Kickstarter doesn't permit them. Here's an example from our campaign, Bubble Hotels.

2. eBikes

It's not that eBikes *won't* work on Kickstarter, but there have been many more highly successful launches on Indiegogo. Here's an example from our campaign, Xion CyberX.

Decision-making time

If your project falls within one of these niche categories, then you know my recommendation.

Otherwise, I have a last decision point to offer here.

STEP 4: WHICH BRAND DO YOUR CUSTOMERS TRUST MORE?

Hear me out on this one. It's important to choose the crowdfunding platform that you believe is more well-known by your customers.

Why?

Because if your customers know the brand of the crowdfunding platform, they will have more trust. More trust usually translates to more sales. So if considering all of these steps still leaves you wondering, then choose the platform you think your customers will trust more.

Wrapping Up

Now you have enough information to decide which platform is best for your own product launch.

The good news is, no matter which you choose, you'll be good. Both platforms are great. There are other aspects of your launch strategy that will cumulatively have more of an effect on its outcome.

CHAPTER

Building a Pricing
Strategy that Converts

Pricing strategy too often becomes an afterthought. There are so many exciting and hands-on tasks to do for a launch, that sometimes the last thing you want to do is immerse yourself in a spreadsheet to figure out your pricing strategy. Deciphering the answers to these important questions isn't the most glamorous part of launching. But it has to be done.

- What discount should I offer?
- How many rewards should I have?
- Should I create a $1 reward?
- Should I have multi-packs?
- Do add-ons and upsells work?

Breathe

I'll answer all those questions and more. In this chapter, I'll teach you the core pricing strategies we use at LaunchBoom, so you'll know what pricing strategy to use for your own launch. And you'll be armed with the tools to build your strategy easily.

Core Pricing Strategies

First, I want to present some high-level concepts we follow for our pricing strategy, which can have a powerful effect when all considered and used together.

DISCOUNTING

We like to define the people's primary motivation for backing crowdfunding projects in one simple sentence:

People look to buy innovative products, at a discount, before anyone else.

This is a core principle of a strategy I like to call "discount stacking." This is where you offer different levels of discounts that expire over time as the campaign goes on. This strategy is most popular in the event ticketing industry.

It's typical for events to have limited "early bird" tickets available at a big discount. When those are gone, a new batch of tickets is available at a slightly worse discount. You can do something similar on your crowdfunding campaign.

PRICE ANCHORING

"Price anchoring" is a cognitive bias where someone's perception of value is based on exposure to an initial price point. If you saw a product for $100 today and then tomorrow you saw the same product for $50, you'd naturally think you were getting a deal on day two. There are ways to use this cognitive bias to drive more conversions.

SCARCITY

A scarce product means that the quantity is limited. With a limited quantity, people are more likely to purchase the product because of fear of missing out (FOMO).

URGENCY

Like scarcity, urgency plays into FOMO, but in this case we're talking about limited time instead of limited quantity.

PARADOX OF CHOICE

Barry Schwartz has a great TED Talk (and a great book) called the "The Paradox of Choice," in which he says:

"[Choice] produces paralysis rather than liberation. With so many options to choose from, people find it very difficult to choose at all."

With this in mind, we strive to *decrease* choice in our pricing strategy, to increase conversion.

VALUE STACKING

As price goes up, so does the value of what's being offered.

Three Pricing Strategies

I recommend different pricing strategies, based on your product offering. Here are three of my favorites.

STRATEGY #1: DISCOUNT STACKING

If you are launching only one product on Kickstarter, I recommend discount stacking. You would offer multiple tiers of rewards, and all of these tiers would sell the same product. The difference is the discount offered for each reward, and the length of time the reward is available.

As an example, let's take a look at how we priced The Empire, which raised $865,235 on Kickstarter and Indiegogo InDemand.

Launch Special—$114

- Quantity limit: 300
- Time limit: beginning of launch until midnight that night

After building a massive prelaunch email list, we started the campaign off with our heaviest discount to reward early backers and drive momentum. For Launch Day, we offered a discount ending at midnight on a limited quantity only, to really incentivize people to grab it before it was too late.

Day 2 Special—$115

- Quantity limit: 150
- Time limit: day 2, until midnight

On the second day of the campaign, we offered another a huge discount – the price was only one dollar higher than on launch day.

Super Early Bird—$119

- Quantity limit: unlimited
- Time limit: day 2 through day 14

After that, we open up a Super Early Bird tier that would only be available until the end of the first two weeks of the campaign.

Early Bird—$125

- Quantity limit: unlimited
- Time limit: day 15 until the end of the campaign

After that was gone, the Early Bird opened up. That discount was the reward planned for the remainder of the campaign.

Kickstarter Special—$155

- Quantity limit: unlimited
- Time limit: entire campaign

We never actually plan to sell the Kickstarter Special. It's only there to serve as a price anchor. That means the Kickstarter Special will always be visible on the page, but there will always be a better discount visible alongside it. The potential backers will be "anchored" by the Kickstarter Special, which makes the more discounted option look even better.

Double Pack—$215

- Quantity limit: unlimited
- Time limit: entire campaign

Four-Pack—$395

- Quantity limit: unlimited
- Time limit: entire campaign

We've found the most popular multi-packs to be two- and four-packs. When pricing these to incentive backers, we aim for a bigger discount than the best single-pack offer.

STRATEGY #2: NO-BRAINER DEAL

If you're selling a product with an add-on that costs you very little to make, but provides a great value to your customer, you can use the "no-brainer deal" strategy.

For example, baKblade 2.0, which raised $1,093,408 on Kickstarter and Indiegogo, had the following items to sell:

- baKblade 2.0
- Four extra blades

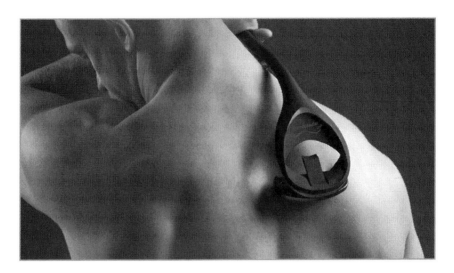

Having the four-pack allowed us to be creative with the bundles we created. The idea we came up with was this:

Starter Pack — $24 (save 30% off retail)

- BaKblade 2.0 (includes two blades)

Full Pack — $29 (save 38% off retail)

- BaKblade 2.0 (includes two blades)
- Four extra blades

The low price of the starter pack was already enticing, but the "Full Pack" was only five dollars more, and an even bigger savings off retail. That enabled us to sell more than three times as many full packs as starter packs. That's what we call a no-brainer deal!

STRATEGY #3: VALUE STACKING

If you have the ability to sell multiple stand-alone products, then I recommend using the "value stacking strategy." In this strategy, as the price goes up, so does the value offered. You can see that it's quite different from discount stacking, where the value goes down as the price goes up (since the discount lessens).

For example, the Alpha Shovel, which raised $192,189 on Kickstarter & Indiegogo InDemand, was able to offer all of the following items:

- Alpha Shovel
- Stealth Shovel
- D-Grip
- Saw with T-Grip
- Stealth Shovel Head

We bundled the items this way:

Alpha Shovel — $99

- Alpha Shovel
- D-Grip

Alpha Pack — $119

- Alpha Shovel
- D-Grip
- Saw with T-Grip

2 Heads Are Better Than 1 — $129

- Alpha Shovel
- D-Grip
- Stealth Shovel Head

Shovel Collection — $169

- Alpha Shovel
- D-Grip
- Stealth Shovel

Whole Enchilada — $189

- Alpha Shovel
- D-Grip
- Stealth Shovel
- Saw with T-Grip

Each bundle offered progressively more value to the backers, which allowed us to raise a significant amount of money for each one of these rewards.

You can download the *Reward & Pricing Template* that we use for planning our rewards, by scanning the QR code or going to crowdfundedbook.com/pricing.

UPSELLING WITH ADD-ONS

Both Kickstarter and Indiegogo have a feature called "add-ons." These are special rewards that allow you to upsell your customers after they choose your campaign's core product. If you use this feature (which I think you should), an add-on product will appear on the "cart" page of either Kickstarter or Indiegogo.

Add-ons allow you to keep your reward pricing simple. Instead of listing every combination of the products you're offering on your crowdfunding page, you can keep the rewards focused on your core product. Once a backer on your crowdfunding page selects your core product, we like to say that you've gotten their "foot in the door." From there, you can upsell them more products using add-ons.

Here's what that looks like for Kickstarter:

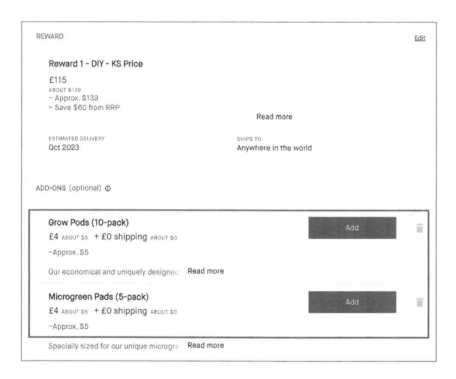

Indiegogo presents it a bit differently.

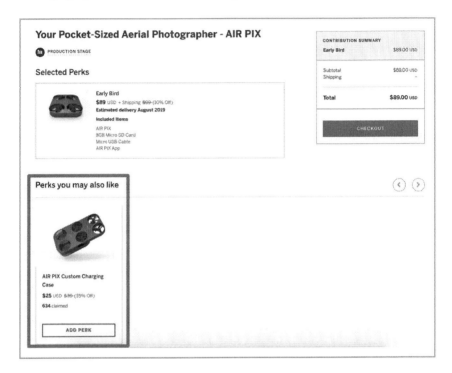

The Indiegogo example is from our AIR PIX campaign, which made $1,611,854 in presale revenue. The add-on we made available was a Custom Charging Case, from which we took in an additional $144,589 in sales. That's nearly a 10 percent lift, just by offering one add-on as an upsell.

Whether it's Indiegogo or Kickstarter, the add-on perk works extremely well.

Here are a few best practices when setting them up:

- **The best add-ons complement your core product.** Choose add-ons that are accessories for your core product or that upgrade it in some way. For AIR PIX, the Custom Charging Case added value to the core product.
- **Limit the number of add-ons to five, maximum.** Remember the "paradox of choice"? When people have too many options,

many times they choose nothing at all. Keep it simple – restrict choices, and only focus on the most high-value add-ons.

- **Keep the price of the add-on lower than the price of the core product.** Including an add-on with a higher price than the core product negatively impacts conversion rates.

Add-ons are an incredibly easy way to increase your overall funding. In the case of AIR PIX, our one add-on increased the overall funding by nearly 10 percent.

Create a High-Converting Pricing Strategy

A high-converting pricing strategy for your campaign is now in your power. Remember, don't try to reinvent the wheel. Use the core pricing strategies I presented here and fill in the template we created for you. Take the time to think this through now and you'll thank yourself later.

CHAPTER

Shipping Your Product

Even though shipping may come after your campaign, you should figure it out before you launch. Don't procrastinate. I've seen too many great campaigns turn into horror stories, all because their shipping strategy was "I think it's good enough."

Let's not let your story be a horror story.

Here's What You Should Consider Prelaunch

PACKAGING

Thinking about packaging isn't the most exciting prospect for everyone. However, being strategic about it will not only help your product arrive at your backer's address in perfect condition, but strategic planning can actually lower costs as well.

If you're new to shipping, it's worth noting that express couriers measure both deadweight and dimensional (or volumetric) weight of a package, and charge the higher of the two. Dimensional weight is calculated by multiplying the length, width, and height of a package and dividing it by a cubic divisor – a number set by each carrier to calculate dimensional weight.

Let's take UPS as an example. If a 24" × 12" × 12" box has a dead-weight of 3 pounds, its dimensional weight would equal 25 pounds. This is based on UPS' dimensional weight calculation of L×W×H / 139 (where 139 is UPS' cubic divisor). This box would be billed as if it weighed 25 pounds even though its deadweight is 3 pounds.

That's why it's important to have packaging that not only protects your product, but is efficient in terms of dimensions. The smaller, the better!

WEIGHT

Because weight has the biggest effect on the shipping cost, your first step is to figure that out. I'm talking total weight, including the box and packaging material.

Since packaging can play into the weight calculations, once you figure out the package you'll use, you may want to consider taking your packaged product to the post office for an accurate weight measurement.

Once you know how much everything weighs, you can start looking into where you're planning to ship.

LOCATION

Location, location, location! While this phrase is usually associated with real estate, it could also be applied to shipping worldwide.

Spoiler alert: not all countries are easy to ship to.

For example, India requires more personal documentation from the receiver than most countries do, and if the receiver doesn't provide this information, your package will be returned. When shipping to Brazil, multiple taxes and duties are imposed on imports. Add that to Brazil's current economic instability, and delivery is even more complicated.

Then there are countries and zones that are considered to be remote areas, and if you decide to ship there, extra fees will apply. Iceland and the Channel Islands are a couple of examples.

When in doubt, ship to fewer countries. Believe me, getting one order from a remote country will likely not be worth it. I recommend starting with the ten most popular countries for crowdfunding, and figuring out your shipping strategy for them first.

These are the ten:

- United States
- United Kingdom
- Canada
- Australia
- Germany
- France
- Sweden
- Japan
- Netherlands
- Singapore

This does not mean you can't or shouldn't ship outside of the list above. But these are a great starting point.

TAXES AND DUTIES

When shipping internationally, it's important to take into account the taxes and duties that could be levied when you import your product to other countries. Those assessments vary by country, which can make it a bit challenging when trying to figure out your shipping budget.

The good news is that tools exist that help you estimate these costs. Easyship, a global shipping software solution, has a tool that shows you the exact amount of import taxes, VAT (value-added tax), GST (goods and services tax), and other fees for every country.

If you'd like to start researching tax and duty rates, Easyship's Countries page has detailed tax, duty, and customs information to help you get started. Check it out by scanning the QR code or going to <u>crowdfund-edbook.com/shipping</u>.

PRODUCTS WITH BATTERIES

Products with batteries can pose a challenge for shipping, as certain batteries (such as lithium ion, stand-alone power packs, and disconnected batteries) are considered "dangerous goods" for couriers.

Dangerous goods can impose an additional cost with some couriers, and cheaper options may not be available. Also, not all companies have the certifications required to ship these kinds of goods, so when getting quotes, this is definitely something you should ask potential couriers about.

Be prepared to get any other relevant certifications for your products, such as an SDS (Safety Data Sheet) or a UN 38.3 (a transportation test for lithium batteries).

If you can't ship your product without batteries, you will need to research each courier's shipping limits for dangerous goods, which can frequently change. Don't even think about *not* mentioning batteries in your shipment's paperwork, as you can be slapped with large fines from governments that are cracking down on undeclared dangerous goods shipments. (There's also the possibility that your product might be destroyed by the courier, if they were not aware that your shipment needed special handling.) Just follow the laws. Otherwise, the risk isn't worth it.

FULFILLMENT

Let's say your campaign is wildly successful and you have to ship out hundreds – or even thousands – of packages to your backers. You should consider working with a fulfillment center to pack everything professionally and ship your product for you.

If you know where most of your backers are located, it may make more sense to choose a fulfillment center close to your target markets, to cut down on shipping costs.

Separately, if you're interested in cutting warehousing costs as well, also look at nearby fulfillment centers. For example, if your factory is in China, Hong Kong is a warehousing hub and free port, meaning you wouldn't have to pay any import taxes.

When you're researching warehouses, you should also consider the charges involved. Some charge extra for heavy items or multiple SKUs (stock keeping units, pronounced "skews") or impose hidden fees such as inbound charges, which will add up for you. Storage fees can also apply, so you'd need to take this into account when shipping your product to the warehouse. It would be wasteful to pay a high storage fee if your items will only need to be stored for a few days.

COURIER COMPARISON

There are hundreds of couriers in the world, and chances are that you've heard of a few. Some couriers are better than others, and it's useful to compare rates and services if you want to cut costs.

While major couriers such as UPS, FedEx, DHL, and TNT are fast and dependable, keep in mind that there are also regional couriers that might provide cheaper rates.

If you're using a fulfillment center, you'll have more options. Depending on weight and volume, and where you're sending your packages, you might be able to save some money by going with a carrier that uses local services for the last mile. But there are times you'll just have to bite the bullet and go for the door-to-door servicers like DHL and FedEx.

How Shipping Works on Kickstarter and Indiegogo

The built-in features for shipping on both Kickstarter and Indiegogo have never been extremely robust. For campaign backers, the experience is not like checking out on an e-commerce store.

On Kickstarter and Indiegogo, the most granular you can get with shipping rates is breaking them down by country. At first glance, that may seem sufficient. But shipping rates to locations within a country can vary widely, especially a big country like the US.

For example, the cost of shipping to New York is dramatically different than shipping to Hawaii. In the case where your only option is one flat rate for an entire country, you essentially have to make an estimate of what you think the average will be, so you can make sure you're not losing money.

The overall amount you raise includes shipping fees. That means the platform fees will apply to the money you collected for shipping, too.

Because of the lack of granularity and fees associated with charging for shipping during a campaign, many creators are now charging for shipping post-campaign.

Charging for Shipping after the Campaign Ends

It's possible to charge for shipping after your crowdfunding campaign ends. Over time, more creators have chosen this path because it's less risky. And with advances in software, the tools that are now available make it easy, as well.

There are three steps you'll need to take if you want to go this route.

1. COLLECT COUNTRY INFORMATION

Even if you aren't charging for shipping during the campaign, you should have backers choose the country that you will eventually be shipping to. Instead of selecting "no shipping involved," select the countries you plan on shipping to, and charge "$0" on Kickstarter. Having this information will be helpful after the campaign.

2. TELL YOUR BACKERS WHEN THEY'LL BE CHARGED

Make it very clear on your campaign materials that shipping will be charged *after* the campaign. If you don't do this up front, you'll have a lot of angry and confused customers.

This needs to be clarified in two places. The following is an example from our campaign, SplatterDōm, which raised $85,940 CAD on Kickstarter.

First, include that information in the reward message.

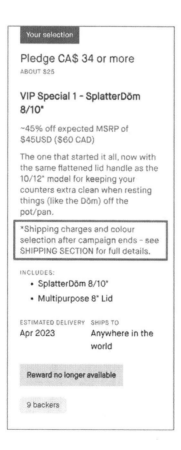

Second, leave a message in the "shipping" section of your campaign page.

SHIPPING & POST CAMPAIGN

| Estimated Shipping Cost Per Country | | |
All estimates provided by a leading logistics company & assume shipping from USA (subject to majority of backers geographic location)		
	Single unit rate starting from	2 unit rate starting from
USA	Depending on which zone $7 - $10	Depending on which zone $8 - $13
Canada	$15.88	$20.88
Australia/New Zealand; Mainland Europe/UK; Caribbean; Americas; Singapore; South Korea; Japan	$18.88	$30.88

3. BE HONEST

Even when you launch, not everything has to be set in stone. It's okay to offer ranges or estimates. The key is to be honest and transparent. It will pay off in the end and save you a lot of headaches.

How to Charge for Shipping Post-Campaign

The most common way to charge for shipping post-campaign is by using a pledge manager. This is software that imports the orders from your campaign and makes the management of your backers' shipping information easy. Think of a pledge manager as your post-campaign hub to make shipping to your backer simple.

In a later chapter, we'll review how to use pledge managers. But for now, just know that you can use them to charge for shipping post-campaign.

Time to Get Ship Done

While all of this is a lot to consider, believe me when I say that taking the time to think about it is time well spent. Hashing out these details will save you from lots of headaches and logistical nightmares down the road. So instead of a horror movie, your campaign will be… whatever the opposite of a horror movie is :)

CHAPTER

Setting Your Funding Goal

At first glance, setting the funding goal for your crowdfunding campaign appears to be a straightforward task. Shouldn't it be the amount you need to create your product?

Perhaps surprisingly, the answer to this question is increasingly becoming "no" for many campaigners. That has to do with their campaign objective.

I'll explain.

Kickstarter and Indiegogo have evolved past the ideas they were founded on. Even though each platform will prominently state that they are not a store, the platforms are still being treated like any other e-commerce platform. This has attracted companies who have realized crowdfunding is more than just a strategy to acquire funds: crowdfunding is now looked on as part of a comprehensive marketing strategy.

WHAT IS YOUR CAMPAIGN OBJECTIVE?

Your campaign objective is how you define success for your campaign. To help identify what it is more precisely, we'll start with some questions.

- What are the fixed costs to create your product? (These include the cost of minimum order quantity, molds, tooling, etc.)
- If you lost money on the crowdfunding campaign, would you still go through with creating your product?
- If yes, how much are you willing to lose?
- What's more important to you: showing a high amount raised on your campaign *or* obtaining the funds to create your product?

With the answers to these questions in hand, ask yourself which of these two strategies you identify with more:

- **Funding strategy** — If I don't hit my funding goal on Kickstarter or Indiegogo, then I won't create my product.
- **Marketing strategy** — I already have the funds to create my product, or I have other ways to get the funds to create my product. Kickstarter or Indiegogo will be my way of getting mass exposure for my product.

To be clear, these two paths are not mutually exclusive. Crowdfunding can both be a funding strategy *and* a marketing strategy, but it's important to know which one is the primary driver in your decision to crowdfund.

CROWDFUNDING AS A FUNDING STRATEGY

If you identify more with crowdfunding as a *funding* strategy, you should choose a funding goal that is the minimum amount required to create your product. Nothing fancy here. If you don't hit that funding amount, you won't create your product.

CROWDFUNDING AS A MARKETING STRATEGY

If you identify more with crowdfunding as a *marketing* strategy, you should choose a funding goal you believe you can reach within twenty-four hours.

Getting funded quickly has its advantages.

- **Increased buyer confidence.** Many backers hold off on supporting projects that aren't funded. The Moment 2.0 creators had a goal of $500K and reported that "between $300–500K we heard from a lot of potential backers who were going to wait until we crossed the funding line. Pick too low and you won't have enough money to deliver. Choose too high and you risk losing momentum and worsening conversion rates."
- **Press coverage is easier.** Crowdfunding campaigns sometimes have a bad rap in the press because of high-profile projects that failed. As a result, getting top-tier media to cover your project is becoming more difficult, so when you aren't funded yet, you'll have an even greater challenge getting coverage.
- **More traffic from the crowdfunding platform.** If you reach your goal quickly and become very well-funded, you will be high in the popularity rankings on the platforms, giving you access to free traffic.

CHOOSING A FUNDING GOAL YOU CAN HIT QUICKLY

To know where you should set your funding goal so you can hit it in twenty-four hours, you need to understand how much traffic you'll be able to send to the campaign within that time frame. As you already know, the top sources of traffic will be your prelaunch email list, online advertising, PR, and the crowdfunding platforms.

Of course, your prelaunch email list will be responsible for most of the sales during the campaign's first twenty-four hours. If you can predict how many sales will come from this channel, you can set your funding goal accordingly.

You can use the predictive model described in the "Adopting a Testing Mindset" chapter to predict how much you'll raise from your email list. Whatever that number is, set your funding goal a little lower.

Here's a link to the TestBoom Predictive Model again: <u>crowdfunded-book.com/testboom</u>.

Remember...

Never choose a funding goal that is lower than what you need. Don't let all this talk about strategically setting your funding goal low cloud your judgment. In the end, you've got to set a funding goal that will allow you to create your product.

Might seem kind of silly to have to say that, but I've seen creators take a huge risk by setting their goals lower than what they actually needed. Worse yet, there was no funding back-up plan. As you can imagine, things didn't end well for them. Let's not have that happen to you!

CHAPTER 23

Choosing When to Launch

$\mathbf{O}$ne of the most common questions I hear (aside from which platform to launch on) is, "When should I launch my crowdfunding campaign?" By *when*, people mean the best month of the year, day of the week, and time of day to maximize their launch results.

To be able to answer this question, we analyzed data from 342,287 Kickstarter projects. The analysis breaks down the data even further than month, day and time of day, by adding two metrics:

- Number of campaigns launched
- Average backers / project

Even though we report on both, the more important metric of those two is average number of backers per project. It does a better job of showing the likelihood that someone will back during a specific time frame.

And even though this data is from Kickstarter projects only, I see no reason why this wouldn't apply to Indiegogo as well.

Alright, let's dive in!

What's the Best Month to Launch?

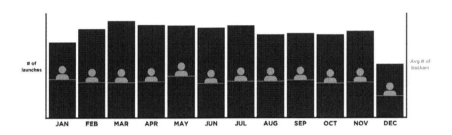

Each bar in the chart above represents one month. The higher the bar, the more projects were launched in that month. The higher the backer icon, the more backers / project there were in that month.

Key insights:

- December is the worst month to launch
- March has been the most popular month to launch campaigns
- May sees more backers per project than any other month

Our analysis is that on average, the best month to launch is May – but only by a small margin compared to the rest of the months (excluding December).

According to the data, you can feel confident launching in any month other than December.

If your product is seasonal, launch during the appropriate season. For example, if you were launching a portable AC unit, you'd want to launch in the summer when it's hot. Don't launch early, in the hope of ensuring that backers receive your product in the month they'd want to use it. This may seem counterintuitive, but people buy products based on the needs they have *now* – even if the product will arrive much later.

What's the Best Day of the Week to Launch?

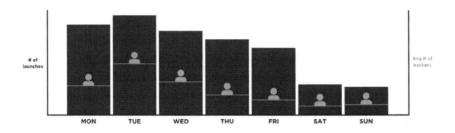

Each bar in the chart above represents one day. The higher the bar, the more projects were launched on that day. The higher the backer icon, the more backers / project were seen on that day.

Key insights from our data:

- Never launch on a weekend
- More projects launch at the beginning of the week
- Tuesday shows the most projects launched and the most backers / project, versus any other day

Tuesday is the best day to launch, on average.

Without even looking at the data, Tuesday makes logical sense. Monday is the start of most people's work week. Since people take some time to get back into "work" mode after the weekend, Mondays can be more hectic than other days. By Tuesday, people are starting to settle into their productive work schedule and are more likely to buy.

We also see higher email-open rates on average on Tuesdays, which is another reason why I think Tuesdays are such a big day.

What's the Best Time of Day to Launch?

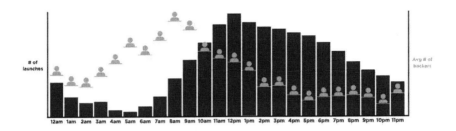

Each bar in the chart above represents one hour in a 24-hour day. (Note that our data reflects EST, Eastern Standard Time.) The higher the bar, the more projects were launched in that hour. The higher the backer icon, the more backers / project were seen in that hour.

Key insights from our data:

- The beginning and end of the day are the worst times to launch projects
- More projects launch around noon EST, compared to any other hour
- The most backers / project come in at 8AM EST

On average, the best time to launch is 8AM EST.

Our analysis is that earlier-in-the-day launches are better because that gives the entire US market (which is the largest crowdfunding market) time to take advantage of your day one sales. It also gives you time to be showcased as "new and noteworthy" on the platforms before most projects launch around noon EST.

Let's Put It All Together!

According to the data, you should launch your campaign…

At 8AM EST on a Tuesday.

You'll notice I didn't specify the month. That's because the most important stats to look at are time of day and day of the week. The month isn't as important as long as you **don't launch in December**.

I've seen many campaigns rush to hit a launch date in a certain month, and end up hurting their success by doing so. It's more important to take the right amount of time to prepare your launch than it is to hit a specific month (again, unless it's a seasonal product).

CHAPTER

24

Preparing for Launch

In the weeks leading up to your launch, there are a few important items to resolve. And if you've followed the strategy up until this point, your bouts of panic regarding your launch should be at a minimum. So let's gear up, because *this rocket is about to launch.*

Submitting for Approval

KICKSTARTER

If you're launching on Kickstarter, you'll need to submit your campaign for approval. **Do this at least one week before your launch day.**

The most common reasons that campaigns **do not** make it past approval are that they don't:

- Clearly show the product and its ability to perform the stated claims, through unedited video on the page
- Present a functional prototype on the page

- Use real photos, but instead provide photorealistic renderings of the product

For most people, getting past this process only takes a few business days, but I've seen it get in the way of launching on time. Avoid this problem by submitting as early as you can. Also know that you can make changes to your campaign page after you submit it, *and* after it has been approved.

INDIEGOGO

If you're launching on Indiegogo, you don't need to submit your campaign for approval. That means that when you press the launch button, your campaign will be live. You'll still have to adhere to Indiegogo's rules, so make sure you are in compliance before you go live.

Build Hype with Email Marketing

Once you have a large enough prelaunch email list to launch, it's time to build up the hype. There are two emails you'll be sending to your list: (1) the launch announcement email, and (2) the launch reminder email. You'll send slightly different emails to your VIP and non-VIP lists.

VIPS

Seven days before you launch, send your VIPs a launch announcement email and touch on the following main points:

- The exact date and time of the launch
- Reminder of the exclusive deal they will receive for being a VIP
- A link to a preview of your campaign page (you can generate a preview link on both Indiegogo and Kickstarter)

Here's what it looked like for our campaign, Top Shelf Camera Bag, which raised $1,185,228 on Kickstarter and Indiegogo InDemand.

BEVISGEAR

Hey there,

It's Matthew from Bevis Gear Inc. and I've got some GREAT news!

Our Top Shelf Camera Bag will be **LAUNCHING on Kickstarter next Tuesday, 12th of June at 7AM PT!**

And since you put down $1 to reserve your Top Shelf Camera Bag, you are going to get something **extra special** when we launch.

On the first day, we will be opening the campaign up to our VIPs (that's you!) **one hour before everyone else!** That means the general public will be notified about our campaign at 8AM PT, giving you 1 hour to grab your VIP discount before everyone else.

Also, want a sneak peek of our campaign page? Click the button below to see our preview link, but please don't share it with anyone! You can ask questions directly on the page and we'll answer them before we launch!

SEE A SNEAK PEEK OF THE CAMPAIGN

Twenty-four hours before you launch, send your launch reminder email. The main points you referenced earlier should be touched on again.

Here's what it looked like for Top Shelf Camera Bag.

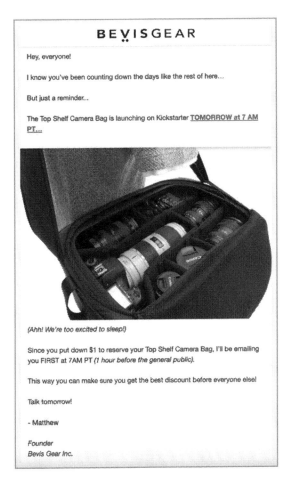

NON-VIPS

Seven days before you launch, send your non-VIPs the launch announcement email and touch on the following main points:

- The exact date and time of the launch
- Reminder that if they upgrade to VIP, they will be able to take advantage of the best deal

This was the Top Shelf Camera Bag launch announcement.

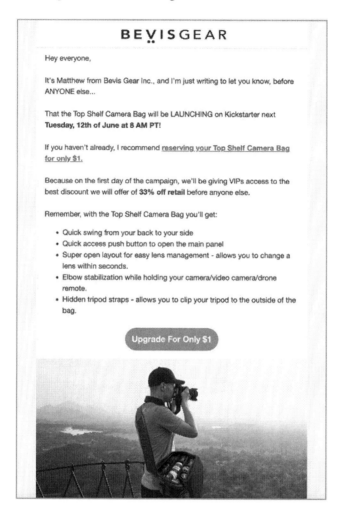

Twenty-four hours before you launch, send your launch reminder email. The main points you cited earlier should be touched on again.

Here's what it looked like for Top Shelf Camera Bag.

It's Time for Liftoff

Congratulations on getting this far! By this point, you've put a great deal of hard work into your campaign and it's about to pay off. And if you've followed all the steps correctly, your campaign is highly likely to get funded quickly after you launch.

As I've been saying, your email list should be the primary driver of revenue to your campaign over the first twenty-four hours. But that doesn't mean you can't drive revenue via other sources. I also recommend focusing on one more special channel while preparing to launch – friends and family.

Don't be afraid to reach out to them personally and ask them to commit to backing your project on day one. Even if they back the campaign at just one dollar, it will help your campaign get higher up in the rankings, which will give it a higher chance of success.

So, with all the preparations complete, there's only one thing left to do: *Launch*.

PART 5:
LAUNCHING A SUCCESSFUL CAMPAIGN

CHAPTER

Having a LaunchBoom

Launch Day! The day you've been dreaming about for so long is near! The day you finally get to click the launch button and become *Crowdfunded!*

With all the prelaunch preparation completed, you should be able to achieve a LaunchBoom, and get funded in the first twenty-four hours.

Pressing the Launch Button

I remember the very first time I pressed the launch button. It felt like pure anxiety was pumping through my veins. I was second-guessing all my tactics and strategies. But once I pressed the launch button, there was an incredible surge of excitement. I knew that all the work of the prelaunch was about to pay off.

That said, there are some things that you want to double-check right before you press the launch button, because they can't be changed once you go live.

1. The campaign duration
2. The campaign funding goal

Once you confirm that your information for these is indeed correct, press that launch button! Your campaign will immediately be live, and you can start to share the link wherever you'd like.

I suggest that you officially launch the campaign one hour before you plan to start marketing it. That gives you the opportunity to share it with friends and family, get some initial funding showing up, and you can make sure everything works before you send it to your community.

Emailing Your Community

I may sound like a broken record at this point, but I'll say it one more time: your prelaunch email list should be the main driver of revenue in the first twenty-four hours of your campaign. You've most likely spent a big chunk of your ad budget building this email list, so it's time to start generating revenue.

Only a portion of your entire email list is going to convert into being customers. On average, 30 percent of VIPs will back the campaign, as will 1 percent of non-VIPs.

The conversion rate usually varies based on your product's price point. (For example, if you have a $1,000 product, your email list is likely going to convert at a lower rate than if you have a $50 product.)

Most people who are going to convert will do so within the campaign's first week. That's why it's important to have an aggressive email strategy during this window.

Besides the first week of the campaign, the next-highest converting portion of the campaign is the final week. The first and final weeks of the campaign are most effective at converting visitors because potential backers feel more urgency to take advantage of limited-time deals.

LAUNCH EMAIL SEQUENCE

During the campaign's first week, you'll be sending many emails to your VIPs and your non-VIPs. Let's look at those.

Email 1: Launch day, morning

Send at: 11AM EST on day 1 (send to VIPs first and send to non-VIPs one hour later at 12PM EST)

- Announce the launch of your campaign.
- Focus on the limited time discounts that are available on day 1.

Email 2: Launch day, evening

Send at: 8PM EST on day 1

- Update VIPs and non-VIPs on the success of your campaign so far, with something like: *We've raised $X from Y number of backers!*
- Remind them that the limited-time discount is still available – but not for long.

Email 3: Day 2

Send at: 11AM EST on day 2

- Update your lists on the success of your campaign so far: *We've raised $X from Y number of backers!*
- Give them the good news that you've added a new reward/perk that is still heavily discounted (though not as good as on the day before).

Email 4: Reason #2

Send at: 11AM EST on day 3

- Share the #2 reason that backers chose to back your campaign.
- Let your people know that you'll share the #1 reason in a few days.
- Remind them of the current best discount they can take advantage of.

Email 5: Reason #1

Send at: 11AM EST on day 5

- Share the #1 reason why backers chose to back your campaign.
- Remind them of the current best discount they can back.

Email 6: Week One Recap

Send at: 11AM EST on day 7

- Recap how much you have raised and how many backers you have after one week of being live on Kickstarter/Indiegogo
- Identify the current best discount that readers can back.

Six emails in a week may seem like a lot, but this works very well. You create real urgency for your email list to back your campaign within the first week, since the discounted tiers will run out. After you've gone through this sequence, I recommend holding off on emailing your list anymore, until the last week of your campaign.

I know this was a very high-level overview, but if I were to include every suggested email in this book, your eyes might begin to glaze over. And, as you've probably guessed, I have templates for you.

You can download our *Launch Emails Template* by scanning the QR code or going to crowdfundedbook.com/email.

EMAIL PEOPLE ONE-TO-ONE

During the prelaunch, it's highly likely that people who signed up for your email list responded to one of your automated emails. That means you have a direct line of communication open with them. Once you launch, I recommend taking advantage of it.

You can email them within the thread that they responded to. Don't worry – I'm aware that you may be wondering why you'd do this, since we just reviewed an entire launch email sequence.

The reason is simple. By emailing people directly, there is a much larger probability that your email will be read. Generally, promotional emails sent from tools like Mailchimp will be filtered by Gmail and other providers into folders marked as "promotion." But when you email someone directly, you bypass that filter.

The one-on-one emails won't be a huge driver of revenue, but I've found them to work fairly well and drive some extra revenue during the first few days. If nothing else, they allow you to continue to build a relationship with potential customers.

Offering the VIP Deal

One of the benefits VIPs get for signing up is that they are guaranteed the best deal possible. How you allow backers to take advantage of this works a little differently on Kickstarter versus Indiegogo.

KICKSTARTER

On Kickstarter, there isn't any way to create an exclusive reward for the VIPs, because every reward you create will be public and available to everyone. Depending on the VIP offer you choose, there are a few ways to message this.

If you go with the "Exclusive Add-On" VIP offer, then your backers can choose anything they want when you go live. Let them know that when you ship your product, their exclusive add-on will automatically be added to their order for free. The ease of management for the product creator is a huge benefit of this type of VIP offer.

If you go with the "Guaranteed Best Discount" VIP offer, then you'll want to create a reward called "VIP Special." This reward will technically be open to everyone. We like to announce the launch of the campaign to the VIPs an hour before everyone else, so they get first access.

If someone on the VIP list forgets to purchase before the VIP tier runs out, we honor their VIP discount by refunding them the difference after the campaign ends. Kickstarter lets you give partial refunds through their backend. It's not as much of a hassle as you may think. Honoring the VIP discount regardless of when they back the campaign is good business.

INDIEGOGO

On Indiegogo, you can use the "secret perk" feature. A secret perk is only visible if people click on a specific link, which means that the perk will not be visible to the general public. I recommend creating a secret perk for VIPs, so you can send them directly to their exclusive discount through email.

Meta Advertising

Once you go live with your campaign, you'll want to turn on Meta advertising as soon as you can. There are three distinct phases to Meta advertising during the campaign:

- Phase 1: Use remarketing to drive extremely high return on ad spend at launch.
- Phase 2: Use best-performing audiences from your prelaunch to drive cold traffic.
- Phase 3: Change the messaging of the ads so consumers will feel driven by urgency, since the campaign will be ending soon.

In phase 1, using remarketing to drive sales will give you an extremely high return on ad spend. Let's dive into how to do this.

PHASE 1 ADVERTISING

Remarketing is when you target audiences that have previously interacted with your brand in some way. During phase 1, there are a few remarketing audiences I recommend targeting.

- VIPs: everyone who signed up for your email list during prelaunch and put down a deposit
- Non-VIPs: everyone who signed up for your email list during prelaunch and did *not* put down a deposit
- Web traffic: everyone who visited your website but didn't opt-in during prelaunch

The reason these audiences are much more likely to yield high return on ad spend is that they are simply more qualified. That's one of the main reasons you want to target them during launch.

The second reason is that you want to create what I call the "surround-sound effect." From their email to their social media feed, people should see your product everywhere they go.

Here's an example of a phase 1 ad for our campaign, VAVA 4K Laser Projector, which raised $2,147,467 on Indiegogo. This ad directly targeted the VIPs.

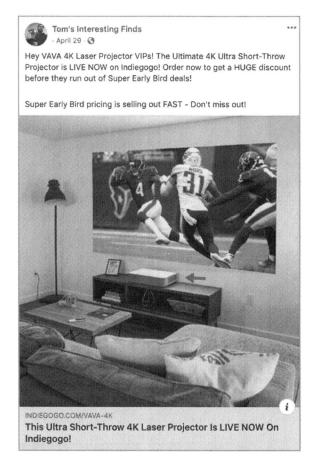

Here's the copy from the ad.

Hey VAVA 4K Laser Projector VIPs! The Ultimate 4K Ultra Short-Throw Projector is LIVE NOW on Indiegogo! Order now to get a HUGE discount before they run out of Super Early Bird deals!

Super Early Bird pricing is selling out FAST - Don't miss out!

By starting the ad copy with "Hey VAVA 4K Laser Project VIPs," we were speaking directly to the audience we were targeting. This made the ad much more effective, as was seen by the direct return on ad spend of 30.12×. That's right: we spent $3,569.27 on this ad, and tracked $107,509 in sales.

BUILDING THE AUDIENCES

You can create these audiences in Meta by going to the Audiences tab in your Meta Ads Manager. Once there, click on "Create Audience" and choose "Custom Audience."

For the VIP and non-VIP audiences, you can upload the email lists directly into Meta and it will create the audiences.

For the web traffic audience, you can choose "Website" as a source and use Meta's targeting options to choose people who visited the site, and exclude those who opted in.

TURNING ADS ON

I recommend waiting two or three hours after your campaign launches to turn these ads on. You'll want to get some traction from your email list first. That early traction will add credibility to the campaign and make visitors from your ad traffic more likely to buy. Simply put, more funding equals more credibility.

We end phase 1 once the ads begin to become unprofitable, which typically happens two to three days after the campaign launches. If this surprises you, just remember that these remarketing audiences are very small.

You're Launched!

This has been quite the journey so far, and this is the final milestone! Once your product is launched, and if you have followed the system up all the way through, you should hit your crowdfunding goal quickly. You are then a *Crowdfunded* Creator.

The journey, however, goes on. It's time to build on this success, continue the momentum, and boost your campaign.

CHAPTER

Live Campaign Advertising

Once you've gotten through your phase 1 advertising, it's time to move on to the next phase that's creatively named... phase 2 advertising. (Shocking, I know.)

Instead of focusing on remarketing to audiences from your prelaunch, it's time to target much larger audiences with the goal of scaling your advertising spend. The strategy will be the same whether you're on Kickstarter or Indiegogo.

Let's start with audiences.

Audience Targeting

During phase 1, your audiences were all remarketing audiences, meaning you were targeting people who had interacted with your brand in prelaunch. In phase 2, you'll be expanding your reach to target a much larger group. Here are the audiences I recommend:

- Lookalikes of your VIPs
- Lookalikes of your email opens
- Strongest interest audiences from the prelaunch

LOOKALIKE AUDIENCES

To generate the Lookalike audiences you'll target, you'll need to go into Mailchimp (or whichever email marketing tool you're using). You'll want to download two segments:

1. Your VIPs
2. Everyone who opened an email from you

Take these two lists and upload them into Meta to create your Lookalike audiences.

INTEREST AUDIENCES

Look back at your prelaunch ads. Find the audiences (1) that drove the most reservations, (2) at the lowest cost per reservation. These are your strongest interest-based audiences. Use these for phase 2.

Building the Ads

Now let's explore how to build a great ad for phase 2, with regard to both the ad copy and the ad creative.

The examples here are from our campaign for VAVA 4K Laser Projector. Here are the final stats for our phase 2 ads, which performed extremely well:

- Amount spent: $34,817
- Revenue: $519,672
- Return on ad spend: 14.93×

Results like this begin with the ad copy.

AD COPY

Ad copy consists of (1) the primary text, and (2) the headline.

PRIMARY TEXT ——————

HEADLINE ——————

Below are a few high-level tactics we use in our ad copy. You can use a combination of these copy tactics for your primary text and headlines.

- Social proof from funding (amount raised, percent overfunded, time to achieve funding)
- Social proof (customer reviews, testimonials, PR articles)
- Feature hyperbole (explain the best or favorite feature using very strong adjectives that project how superb the product is)

For crowdfunding campaigns, social proof and validation are very important. Because the product doesn't exist yet, there aren't any customer reviews in the way there are on Amazon or other e-commerce sites. Any sort of review from a reputable source, or even just a friend's testimonial, can help alleviate a new customer's concerns around a product that simply doesn't exist publicly yet.

This is another reason that your ads should lean into the social proof from your crowdfunding campaign. For example, you can say things like:

- Funded in 22 minutes!
- Over 352% funded!
- Raised over $532,032!

Here's an example of ad copy that we ran for the VAVA 4K Laser Projector.

Primary Text

This projector is CRAZY! You can literally put it just 7.2" from your screen or wall and project a perfect image onto a 100" screen! It uses the same laser tech movie theaters use and shows videos in 4K!

I hosted movie night with this and whenever people got up I was expecting a giant shadow to disrupt the image, but of course it was fine!

Headline

This INSANE 4K Laser Projector Was 100% Funded On Indiegogo In Just 22 MINUTES!

In this ad, you can see how we used hyperbole with statements like "CRAZY" and "INSANE." We also leaned into social proof offered by the crowdfunding platform with statements like "100% funded" and "just 22 MINUTES."

AD CREATIVE

The ad creative comes between the primary text and headline of your ad, as seen below.

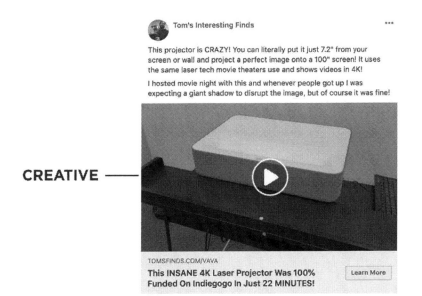

When it comes to ad creative, the same methodology applies as in the chapter "Driving Traffic with Paid Ads." It's typically best to use more authentic imagery versus polished, professional creative. It's fine to use your phone and free tools like Canva to create your ad creative.

To see our "best-of" gallery for live campaign advertising, download the *LaunchBoom Ad Library*. Scan the QR code or go to crowdfundedbook.com/ad-library.

Try It Yourself

As in Phase 1, watch your advertisements closely. If you're getting great returns from the ads, don't be afraid to turn up the budgets. If you're seeing terrible returns from the ads, don't be afraid to turn them off.

If you find all this material about ads overwhelming, you may want to hire an agency to do the ads for you. In the next chapter, I'll discuss hiring agencies and how you should evaluate them. But before you make a decision to work with an agency, I recommend spending at least *some* money on advertising to see what kinds of returns you'll get. Who knows? Maybe it will work. You won't know until you try.

CHAPTER 27

Boosting Your Campaign

The first few days of a campaign are downright exciting. Getting funded after months (maybe years) of hard work is cause for some celebration. Sadly, it's very common for that excitement to die quickly.

You see, most campaigns will enjoy a spike of funding the first few days, and then watch sales drop off to a fraction of what they were before. We lovingly call this period the *valley of death*.

When creators experience the valley of death for the first time, many panic. At about the same time, they'll receive a flood of messages from "experts" promising them the solution to get them out of this slump.

Creators who don't read this book may make a rash decision and pay thousands of dollars to a charlatan. But *you* won't be one of those creators. You'll know which opportunities are worth pursuing, and how to use them to boost your campaign.

Ad Agencies

Many agencies will be happy to manage your ads once your campaign goes live. Unfortunately, many will claim that they'll give you incredible returns, but instead they'll take your money and give you... nothing.

Although it's not necessary to use an ad agency, nearly every one of the top campaigns do. Here's how I recommend finding the right one.

CHOOSE A PERFORMANCE-BASED FEE STRUCTURE

Ad agencies have different ways of charging for their services, and I would only go with an agency that charges a commission based on performance. That means you should avoid agencies that have fee structures that:

- Charge up-front payments
- Charge percentage of ad spend

The agency should provide you with a dashboard that clearly shows the results of their ads on a daily basis. The dashboard should include your conversion rates and ad metrics, most important among them being your ROAS (return on ad spend).

AVOID CONTRACTS YOU CAN'T GET OUT OF AT ANY TIME

Avoid any agency that makes it difficult for you to stop working with them. You want to be able to get out of the contract at *any* time.

If the agency's contract requires you to be exclusively with them for the term of the contract, that should be fine. It's okay to be exclusive to the agency while the contract is active. That's because having two agencies working for you at the same time is not the most efficient strategy. Both agencies would be targeting some of the same audiences, so you'd be wasting some ad spend.

GOOGLE THEM

This may seem self-explanatory, but you may be surprised at how many creators don't bother to do a simple Google search before working with some of these agencies. Because if they did, it's hard for me to believe that they'd have chosen the agencies they're working with.

Type the agency name and "reviews" into Google and make sure that you **scroll down past the first results**. The worst offenders have made their own review sites or they've written review articles about themselves… which is beyond me.

If they don't have legitimate reviews on sites like Google, TrustPilot, etc., then I'd recommend staying away.

OTHER COMMON REQUIREMENTS

Most advertising agencies also have the following requirements as part of their deal:

- **Share your backer list:** Every single agency I've seen requires you to hand over your entire backer list once the campaign is over. They use these email lists to aid in targeting for their future clients.
- **Feature their company on the campaign page:** Most agencies require that you put a banner promoting their company on your campaign page.
- **Access to your campaign:** They'll need access to your campaign to track their sales.

MY LIST OF VETTED AGENCIES

You can also skip all the hard work of vetting agencies and just work with agencies that we've vetted at LaunchBoom.

You can see the current list by scanning the QR code or going to crowdfundedbook.com/experts.

Kickstarter Promotions

Kickstarter does have a few promotional opportunities for your campaign. They aren't exactly easy to take advantage of, but if you do get to use some of them, they can be very effective.

NEWSLETTER

Kickstarter's newsletter can drive a lot of traffic to your campaign. The problem is, it's difficult to get into it. That's because Kickstarter is pretty selective.

Don't let that discourage you from reaching out to them. Start the conversation with the Kickstarter team to see if they can provide you with any extra support. It won't hurt to ask – and you may end up in their newsletter.

PROJECT WE LOVE

Being recognized as a "Project We Love" is highly sought after by every Kickstarter campaign. It used to be called "staff pick." Regardless of the name, the idea is the same. Kickstarter's staff can choose any project on the platform to be a "Project We Love," which gives the project a special badge and better placement on the website.

I know what you're thinking. How do I get myself that badge!? Unfortunately, there isn't a hack to get your campaign this recognition. After talking with staff at Kickstarter, here are the main things to focus on for increasing your likelihood of attaining "Project We Love" status:

- Create a product that is actually innovative and unlike anything the world has seen
- Create a campaign page and video that is very aesthetically pleasing
- Tap your network to see if they know any staff at Kickstarter, and get a direct introduction to someone who works there

FEATURED PLACEMENTS

Kickstarter has featured placements on their website that can drive a lot of traffic to your campaign. The home page banner can be one of the most effective places to be featured. But Kickstarter also has featured placement for each of the category pages that can be effective as well.

Campaigns generally get these placements only if they are a Project We Love first. If you do get that Project We Love recognition, try to speak to Kickstarter's team about any additional placement you can get.

Indiegogo Promotions

Indiegogo has promotional opportunities very similar to Kickstarter's. They are easier to take advantage of, but may be generally less effective.

NEWSLETTER

Indiegogo has an effective newsletter. Not everyone will be featured in their newsletter, but it's easier to get into than Kickstarter's. Indiegogo will often give creators funding thresholds to hit in order to "unlock" newsletter placement. For example, they may tell you that once you reach 50 percent of your funding, you'll get a newsletter placement.

Again, this isn't guaranteed, but if you're launching on Indiegogo, I recommend reaching out to them to talk about their newsletter before you launch.

FEATURED PLACEMENT

Like Kickstarter, there are a few featured placements on Indiegogo's website that will drive traffic to your campaign. The most effective placement they have is in their home page rotating banner.

There are two ways to get into the home page banner.

- **Sponsored placement:** You pay Indiegogo to become a "GOGOPICK." Reach out to their team for details.
- **Popular project:** Your project is so popular on their platform that it's in their best interests to place you in the home page banner so more backers find it. As with newsletter placement, Indiegogo may give you funding milestones you must hit to unlock the home page banner placement.

Backer Newsletters

There are many email newsletters specifically for people interested in crowdfunding products. Some of these work well. Some of these…not so much.

Remember that since this is a book, some of the info (such as pricing) may have changed by the time you read this! To get the most up-to-date list of recommended backer newsletters, scan the QR code or go to crowdfundedbook.com/newsletters.

For now, I recommend looking into the newsletters listed here.

FIRST BACKER

First Backer is a newsletter by Jellop. Jellop's main service is live advertising only on Kickstarter. If you work with them on your ads, then you'll also get access to their newsletter. They charge a commission on funds raised from their newsletter.

BACKERKIT

BackerKit is pledge management software (which we'll cover in a later chapter). They also have a newsletter that can be very effective. The catch is that in order to get in their newsletter, you must commit to using their pledge manager. They charge a commission on funds raised from their newsletter.

PLEDGEBOX

PledgeBox is also pledge management software with a newsletter. It's a good alternative to BackerKit's newsletter because there is no commitment to use their pledge manager. The catch is that they charge an up-front fee *and* a commission.

PRODUCTHYPE

ProductHype is a backer newsletter for more successful projects. As I write this today, your crowdfunding campaign must have raised at least $50K to be considered in the newsletter. Because of the commitment to only the most popular campaigns, sales driven by the newsletter tend to be consistently high. They charge a commission on funds raised from their newsletter.

BACKER...

There seem to be a million different newsletters that have all copied each other named Backer "something" [insert word here]. BackerClub, BackerCrew, BackerLand, you name it.

Almost all of them charge an up-front fee and a commission, but the up-front fee is essentially a prepayment for the commission. So if the commission does not surpass the up-front fee, you don't owe anything additional.

I have rarely found any of these newsletters to be worthwhile. They usually return about the same amount of sales as the up-front fee, which means the creator will lose money after producing the product. I don't recommend any of these knockoffs.

Boost Your Campaign

Remember, almost 100 percent of campaigns experience a drop in daily funding after the first few days. Don't panic. Use the information in this chapter to determine the best option to boost your campaign and keep the momentum going.

CHAPTER

PR and Influencer Strategy

I'll be honest: PR can be a rollercoaster. It *can* be a very effective way to drive revenue and add credibility to a campaign. Alternatively, it can also be a massive money-suck. Unlike Meta advertising, it's notoriously difficult to track the direct return on investment, but that doesn't mean it's devoid of value.

I watched our baKblade 2.0 campaign get picked up by *Business Insider*, go viral, and drive over $200K in sales in just three days. I've also watched clients insist on spending $15K on a PR agency and get a few articles written about them on some no-name websites — essentially flushing $15K down the drain.

In many cases, it's not the PR agency's fault that a product didn't get picked up by more major publications. There are many, many products vying for the attention of these sites. Sometimes it just takes time for them to write about you, or maybe a journalist doesn't think your product is interesting enough.

In all the years of launching campaigns, I've come to the conclusion that you should only invest in a PR agency if you have $10-15K in additional budget that you wouldn't miss if returns were incredibly low.

If you don't have that money to invest, don't worry. I'm not just going to leave you tip-less. Pay attention for the best way to execute on a PR and influencer strategy yourself.

Use Kickbooster

Kickbooster was launched in 2015 by Scott Adamson. I remember it clearly since it was the same time that LaunchBoom began. Scott had reached out to one of our campaigns about his new service that allowed people to create cash-back programs for Kickstarter campaigns.

Intrigued, I signed up for one of our clients and set up a cash-back program. It didn't drive very many sales for the campaign, but I was still interested in what that software could lead to. After many calls with Scott, I learned that Kickbooster's strategy was focused on the long term.

They saw a bigger play than simply creator-run cash-back programs. They sought to create a platform and community of Kickbooster affiliates. By doing that, they'd be able to directly connect big affiliates with creators instead of relying on creators to find the affiliates themselves.

Kickbooster has become a no-brainer for any crowdfunding campaign. Let's dive into the top three reasons why.

1. KICKBOOSTER'S AFFILIATE NETWORK DRIVES REVENUE

Kickbooster has a massive community of affiliates, which they call "boosters." When you set up your project on Kickbooster, you have the option to add your project to their marketplace. I highly recommend you do this, as it makes your project visible to their community of boosters.

We used Kickbooster for our Stealth Wallet campaign that raised $619,411 on Kickstarter and Indiegogo InDemand.

On Kickbooster, they were able to raise $21,795 from 111 boosters.

Every single one of those boosters signed up on their own after finding the project in the Kickbooster Marketplace. Just by clicking one button, we were able to add an additional $21,795 in funding to the campaign. That's not so bad, in my book.

2. KICKBOOSTER IS A NEW WAY TO GET PRESS

Kickbooster did a great job recruiting online publishers to become boosters. The pitch was simple: Write an article about a crowdfunding campaign and get paid a percentage of each sale that comes from your article. This incentivizes publishers to write about projects on Kickbooster — giving the creator additional sales and also the credibility that press provides.

Let's take another look at Stealth Wallet.

Top boosters			
Booster	**Clicks**	Boosts	Boosted
Gizmodo Media Group	8204	89	$7,185
InsideHook	2293	74	$4,074
Man of Many	1892	34	$2,177
Laura Casing	1421	27	$1,919
Backers Today	429	25	$1,326
Saiful Rahman	7542	15	$1,062
Gear Junkie	422	18	$989

The top booster was Gizmodo, a well-known publisher. After that came two more publishers, InsideHook and Man of Many. Because these publishers wrote articles about Stealth Wallet, we were able to put their logos on the campaign, further boosting credibility.

3. KICKBOOSTER IS EXTREMELY AFFORDABLE

The pricing model for Kickbooster is straightforward and affordable. It breaks down as follows:

- $29 per month
- Commission on funds raised through Kickbooster (3 percent goes to Kickbooster + whatever commission rate you decide to pay boosters)

The only fixed cost is the $29 per month. Everything else is variable based on performance.

You can sign up for your own Kickbooster account by scanning the QR code or going to crowdfundedbook.com/kickbooster.

PR Outreach Strategy

If you want to do PR outreach yourself, here's how it's done.

MAKE A PRESS KIT

A press kit is a folder of assets that are super-useful for the press, and it's fairly simple to put together. Create a folder (in something like Google Drive or Dropbox) and make it visible to anyone on the web. Create sub-folders for photos and videos.

For example, this is what our campaign for Hooke Lav, which raised $580,753 on Kickstarter, looked like in Google Drive:

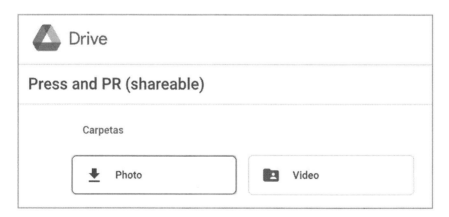

Create a link to the press kit on your campaign page. Here's the graphic we created for Hooke Lav:

If you want to see an example of a press kit, scan the QR code or go to crowdfundedbook.com/presskit.

CREATE AN OUTREACH LIST

The easiest way to create a list of media publications to reach out to is by researching your competitors or similar Kickstarter campaigns. I'll give you a hypothetical example.

Let's say you had a product similar to Hooke Lav. You would go to Hooke Lav's Kickstarter campaign and search for a media logo cloud – this shows all the different media sites that have covered Hooke Lav.

The media logo cloud for Hooke Lav looked like this:

Now you have the names of twelve different media sites (large and small) that you can add to your outreach list. You know that they're interested in your type of product.

Next, find the actual articles that were written about Hooke Lav. For example, if you type in "New Atlas Hooke Lav" into Google, the *New Atlas* article will be at the top of the results.

Click on it.

Look for the name of the journalist who wrote the article.

Now go to LinkedIn and look up the writer. You can send a message from there.

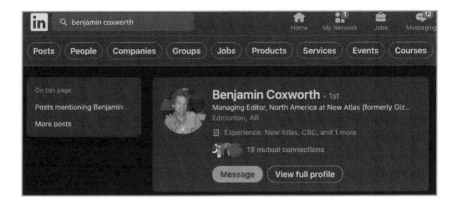

—

Another way to find media sites is through Google.

Continuing with the Hooke Lav example, you'd go to Google and type in *lav mic review*. Then you'd select "News" to filter by media sites that have written about lav mics.

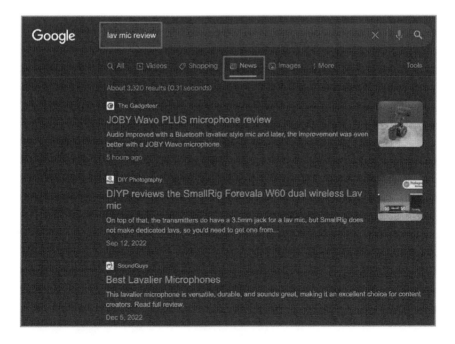

Again, you can create a list of different media sites and journalists that covered similar products.

Finding a journalist who covered a product similar to yours enables you to reach out and pitch them your project.

One more thought: while messaging on LinkedIn can work, it's even better if you get the journalist's email address. I recommend using a tool like https://hunter.io that will allow you to find almost anyone's email address. Their free plan gives you twenty-five searches, so I'd start there.

REACHING OUT

You'll need to craft a pitch to send to the journalists you've identified. You don't want to write a novel, but something too short won't work either. Here's an example of a pitch email for our client Hooke Lav:

–

Hi [name],

I'm reaching out to introduce Hooke Lav – a wearable microphone with studio-quality sound that captures dropout-free audio with one click.

Hooke Lav is a wireless microphone that captures pro-grade sound with no wires, no dropouts, and no hassle. The Bluetooth lav has 8GB of internal storage and connects to any device with the click of a button.

- No latency
- Weight: 10 grams
- Apple MFi certified
- 8GB internal storage
- Headphone/cable slot
- Mobile app integration
- Micro USB charging slot
- iPhone and Android compatible
- 7 hours continuous battery life
- 24bit 48kHz mono and dual channel audio
- Pro-gear compatible with cameras, field recorders, etc.

Here's the Press kit and Kickstarter page, to find all the details.

Would this be something you might be interested in covering?

—

Use this template and adapt it to your product. Send the message to as many different media publications with audiences that you think will overlap with yours.

Lastly, remember that cold outreach is mostly a numbers game. Most people either won't respond or will say no. The more you reach out, the higher the likelihood that you'll get coverage.

Attracting Press Organically

The press writes about what they think people will find interesting. So if your campaign is generating buzz, the likelihood that you will be written about is quite high.

Back in the early days of LaunchBoom, we actually had no press strategy for baKblade 2.0. However, there was so much buzz created by our advertising efforts that *Business Insider* reached out to us because they wanted to post a video to their audience. That video went viral and got over 30 million views on Facebook and spurred literally hundreds of other sites to pick up the campaign. This led to hundreds of thousands of dollars raised in the last few days.

I'm not saying that you are guaranteed press by having a great campaign, but I've seen many creators get wrapped up in outreach strategies instead of focusing on the fundamentals of a great campaign.

Influencer Marketing

Ah, *influencers…* Love them or hate them, they can drive some serious revenue. Here are some quick stats:

- Eight out of ten consumers have purchased a product after seeing it recommended by an influencer (Rakuten Marketing)
- 61 percent of consumers trust influencer recommendations, while only 38 percent trust branded social media content (Shopify)
- People are four times more likely to make a purchase when referred by a friend (Uniqodo)

Clearly, influencer marketing can be very effective overall, but how does it work for crowdfunding campaigns? I'll show you.

DIFFERENT INFLUENCER TYPES

Broadly speaking, there are five different types of influencers that you can leverage for marketing:

- Nano: 1,000 – 9,999 followers
- Micro: 10,000 – 49,999 followers
- Mid-tier: 50,000 – 499,999 followers
- Macro: 500,000 – 999,999 followers
- Mega: 1,000,000+ followers

My recommendation is to skip the Mega, Macro, and Mid-Tier and focus on Micro and Nano influencers, because they:

- Are much easier to reach
- Typically have much higher engagement
- Focus influence on specific topics/industries
- More likely are open to commission agreements

For these reasons, Micro and Nano influencers typically will give you a much higher ROI than any other tier.

CHOOSING THE BEST INFLUENCERS

I like to use something called the "three R's" when looking for influencers.

1. **Relevance:** how much an influencer's audience aligns with your brand/product
2. **Reach:** the number of people who will be exposed to the message
3. **Resonance:** the influencer's ability to drive measurable results with their audience

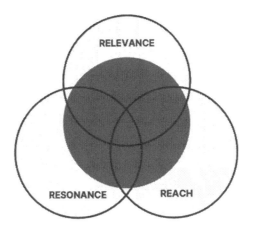

Keep these three R's in mind.

HOW TO FIND THEM

I'm going to give you a hypothetical example to show how I'd find influencers. Let's say that you're launching a new travel backpack. First, I'd suggest starting with YouTube.

YouTube

Search for *travel backpack reviews* on YouTube. Immediately, you'll see a list of different YouTube channels to reach out to.

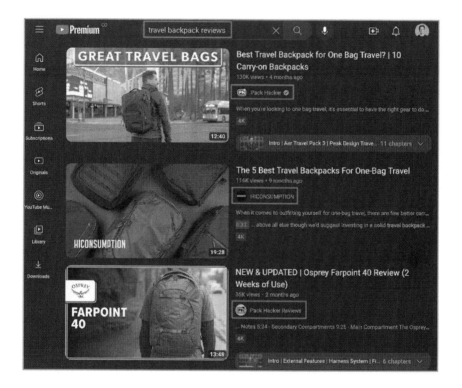

Hashtags

On Instagram and TikTok, type in the hashtag *#travelbackpack*. From there, look up different influencers that used that hashtag.

Brands Meet Creators

There's an awesome free service called "Brands Meet Creators." It's a platform that connects influencers / UGC creators with brands. (UGC stands for user-generated content, also sometimes referred to as "consumer-generated content.") Brands Meets Creators is free to use, so go there and post a listing about your new travel backpack. From there, you'll get a few hundred applications to sort through. Look for the best Micro and Nano influencers with the best mix of the three R's.

Check out Brands Meets Creators by scanning the QR code or going to crowdfundedbook.com/brands.

REACHING OUT

The best method for outreach will depend on which platform you use. For example, a YouTube channel typically lists a business contact in its "About" section. On Instagram or TikTok, DMs can work really well.

Here are some tips to make your outreach more effective.

- Be personal, rather than formal
- Tell them why you think their audience would love your product
- Comment on and compliment their work
- Ask if they're open to collaborating
- Send samples (if possible)

This may be obvious, but rarely will someone cover your product for free. A recent article from Shopify lays out the average influencer costs in 2023. As a baseline, the current industry standard is $100 per 10,000 followers. With that in mind, here's the average cost per post, broken down by the different influencer types.

- **Nano:** $10 – $100
- **Micro:** $100 – $500
- **Mid-tier:** $500 – $5,000
- **Macro:** $5,000 – $10,000
- **Mega:** $10,000+

Nano and Micro influencers are more open to commission-based agreements. I recommend setting up your Kickbooster account and pitching your influencers on getting a commission of every sale they send. Not every influencer will be open to this, but it won't hurt to ask. If they say yes, you'll be able to reduce your risk dramatically.

Wrapping Up

As I mentioned in "The Four Horsemen of Traffic," PR and influencers are important, but they won't drive the most sustained traffic to your campaign. It's important to put some of your focus on them, but don't kill yourself trying to make this work. It can be very hit-or-miss.

At a minimum, set up your Kickbooster account and tap into their marketplace. If you have more in your budget, hire a PR agency to do the outreach for you. And if you want to try the outreach yourself, use the strategy and templates I provided.

CHAPTER

Campaign Updates and Stretch Goals

Keeping your backers engaged during the campaign is important, and there are three main ways to do that. The first is by posting campaign updates, which are broadcast messages sent through the crowdfunding platform. The second is by using stretch goals, which are special benefits that will unlock as the campaign hits certain funding goals. The third is through comments, which backers can leave on your campaign page.

Let's start with campaign updates.

Campaign Updates

Campaign updates are a core feature of both Kickstarter and Indiegogo, enabling you to send a message to every backer at once. You can also choose to make the update public to anyone else who visits your campaign page.

Here's an example from our campaign, Dr. Squatch, which raised $100,429 on Kickstarter. After we got funded, we posted an update to the backers, aptly named "Let's Party."

Are campaign updates really that important? Short answer: yes. Here's why...

■ Campaign updates are the best way to communicate with all your backers at once.

■ You can add cross-promotions to your updates, which opens your campaign up to additional potential backers.

■ Updates keep your community engaged and can help build trust.

HOW OFTEN SHOULD YOU POST?

At a maximum, I'd post once a week during the campaign. That's because it is possible to send *too many* campaign updates. We've seen a direct correlation between canceled pledges and a client sending multiple updates in the same week. That seems to be because (if the campaign is on Kickstarter) updates serve as a reminder that the backer can cancel their pledge before the campaign ends. That's why – and take note of this – I also don't recommend sending *any* updates during the final week of your campaign.

WHAT SHOULD YOU POST?

Share any information you think your backers should be aware of or would find interesting. This may go without saying, but keep the topics related to your campaign. Certain campaign updates get posted on almost every campaign, including topics such as:

- Hitting your funding goal
- Announcing a stretch goal
- Campaign ending and discussion of next steps

Stretch Goals

Stretch goals are unique to crowdfunding. Rewards that unlock when you hit certain self-defined funding goals aren't *necessary*, but they are pretty common and can provide a fun way to engage and reward your backers.

STRETCH GOAL EXAMPLE #1

Here's an example from our campaign for Creed's Codex, which raised $52,277 on Kickstarter.

Stretch Goals

Stretch goals are additional content we'd love to produce in collaboration with our backers. The more funding we get the more content we can create.

$5,000 RAISED   UNLOCKED

UNEARTHED HUMAN RELICS
two all new full page illustrations
voted on by the backers

This is just one of nine different stretch goals that were included on the campaign. For gaming-related campaigns, offering many stretch goals like this one is extremely common.

STRETCH GOAL EXAMPLE #2

Here's an example from our campaign, Give'r Gloves, which raised $270,942 on Kickstarter and Indiegogo InDemand.

First Stretch Goal!

Backers Unite! Complete 4 out of the 5 achievements below and unlock the first stretch goal!

Each pair of 4 Season Gloves will receive a pair of custom Give'r wrist straps - let your gloves hang close by when you have to take them off!

Reach $100K in Funding!

$100k!

50 COMMENTS!

50

50 comments on our Kickstarter campaign page answering the question "What are you most excited to do with your new 4-Season Give'r Gloves?"

8,000 GIVE'R FANS!

Reach 8,000 fans on the Give'r Facebook Page!

10 LOGO RECREATIONS!

10 people recreate the Give'r Mountain Logo and post a picture to our Facebook page!

5 VIDEO SUBMISSIONS!

give'r

5 video submissions to our Facebook Page where Give'r fan, age 8 or under, states "The 4-Season Give'r Gloves are the Best Damn Gloves Ever" - Post the video to our Facebook page!

This is one of two stretch goals that Give'r offered on their campaign. I absolutely love this stretch goal strategy because it's more than just hitting a funding goal. Backers are encouraged to engage and unlock the goal through various methods.

THERE ISN'T ONE WAY TO DO IT

With stretch goals, there isn't *one* right way. You can be as creative as you want.

You also don't *have to* have stretch goals. I want to stress this point, because I've seen creators think they *have to* have stretch goals. That is not the case.

Stretch goals can be a fun way to reward backers for supporting your campaign. But if it's difficult for you to come up with stretch goals, it may be better to just leave them out.

Comments

If someone backs your crowdfunding campaign, they can leave a public comment, and it's important for you to engage with comments quickly and professionally. That's because many potential backers and current backers read comments for any possible red flags.

Responding to comments and addressing concerns in a professional and thorough way will lead to a more successful campaign. Not only will it assist in getting someone to back your campaign, but it can also prevent current backers from canceling.

Engaging with Your Backers

At the end of the day, it matters how you communicate and engage with your backers. I've seen campaigns start strong, but then ignore their backers for the entire campaign. This has led to cancellations and campaigns ending with less funding than the day they launched.

But the good news is that it's not that hard to engage with your backers in a meaningful and effective way. Just follow the tips in this chapter and you'll be all set!

Cross-Promotions

Cross-promotions help drive more sales to your campaign.

There are lots of other live campaigns on Kickstarter, and some of those campaigns have backers who would also be interested in your product.

What if you each promoted the other's campaign in one of your campaign updates? That would probably drive some sales, right?

That's a cross-promotion.

This is essentially a free way to promote your product. The only cost is your time. Here's why it works so well as a promotion tactic.

- **It's email marketing.** When someone promotes your campaign in a cross-promotion, they'll add your campaign at the end of a campaign update. And as you know, when a campaign update is posted, it sends all the backers of that campaign an email. So by getting added to another product's campaign update, you are getting free email marketing delivered to a group of people who may be interested in your product.

- **Third-party endorsement.** When a campaigner agrees to promote you to their backers, you are taking advantage of the trust that campaigner has with their backers.
- **Backers are more likely to purchase.** You know that the people seeing the promotion are willing to purchase a product on a crowdfunding site. The people you're being promoted to are, therefore, very qualified.
- **It's free.** Like I said – the only cost here is your time.

This strategy only works on Kickstarter, though. Indiegogo doesn't let you message campaigns unless you're already a backer of the campaign. On Kickstarter, you just need to have a Kickstarter account and you can send any campaign creator a message.

For that reason, we're going to dive into how to execute these cross-promotions for Kickstarter.

First, it's important to be methodical about your outreach. You'll want to choose campaigns that:

- You genuinely think your backers will like
- Have similar demographics and interests
- Have similar backer counts. (Don't reach out to a campaign with 10,000 backers when you only have 100. It's not a fair trade.)

Okay, let's dive into the process for outreach.

Reaching Out

STEP 1: GO TO KICKSTARTER'S DISCOVER PAGE

Kickstarter's Discover page is where you can search for current campaigns, and also every campaign that's ever been on Kickstarter. Go to Kickstarter's Discover page (https://www.kickstarter.com/discover/advanced) and choose the category your product is in.

STEP 2: REFINE YOUR SEARCH

Refine your search a little more, so your outreach will be more targeted. By clicking on "more filters," you'll find some options to do this. Change from "All" projects to "Live" projects. Then use the "amount pledged" filter to target different size campaigns.

STEP 3: REACH OUT

You can start to reach out to the campaigns that fit within the criteria we've discussed (campaigns that share your target market and have similar backer counts). On the campaign page for a campaign you'd like to reach out to, you can click on the creator's name to open their profile. You'll see a big "Contact Me" button, which is how you'll send them a message.

Here's a simple template for you:

Hey there,

I love the detail and design of your [campaign name or product].

I thought I'd reach out to see if you were interested in doing a cross-promotion where we mention one another's campaigns in an update. I think my backers would love your campaign!

You can check out my campaign here: [your crowdfunding campaign URL].

If you're interested, please send me the link, text, and picture you'd like me to use.

Thanks,

[your name]

Posting Cross-Promotions

You should expect to get responses to your outreach within a day or two. As I noted earlier, I recommend adding cross-promotions at the *end* of your campaign update. That way, you keep the focus of your campaign update on *your* campaign. You don't want to be overly promotional with your backers. I recommend having three cross-promotions, max, in each of your campaign updates.

Here's an example of what a cross-promotion looks like at the end of a campaign update. This is from our campaign for DMOS Alpha Shovel, which raised $177,496 on Kickstarter.

Check out these awesome projects!

The Pocket Samurai - Keychain Knife

Our buddies at StatGear have done it again! This time they've re-introduced their popular Pocket Samurai in an aircraft grade aluminum version. The perfect everyday carry (EDC) pocketknife with a razor sharp blade and iconic Samurai sword style. Check it out here!

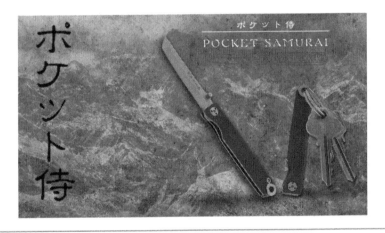

You can see that we promoted the Pocket Samurai campaign to backers of DMOS. In return, Pocket Samurai included DMOS in their campaign update. By the end of the campaign, DMOS had generated $9,519 in additional sales just from cross-promotions. Here's the screenshot from Google Analytics:

Medium	Sessions	% New Sessions	New Users	Bounce Rate	Pages / Session	Avg. Session Duration	Ecommerce Conversion Rate	Transactions	Revenue
	2,158 % of Total: 1.27% (169,580)	72.47% Avg for View: 38.18% (-17.62%)	1,564 % of Total: 1.05% (149,520)	74.14% Avg for View: 87.93% (-15.08%)	1.50 Avg for View: 1.18 (25.59%)	00:01:23 Avg for View: 00:00:27 (214.34%)	3.24% Avg for View: 0.04% (7,70%)	70 % of Total: 0.95% (7,770)	$9,519.00 % of Total: 5.78% ($177,490.15)
1. 109	207 (9.59%)	72.46%	150 (9.59%)	69.57%	1.57	00:01:42	6.76%	14 (20.90%)	$1,808.00 (18.99%)
2. 107	297 (13.76%)	74.41%	221 (14.12%)	71.04%	1.60	00:01:35	3.70%	11 (15.71%)	$1,659.00 (17.43%)
3. 116	254 (11.77%)	79.92%	203 (12.98%)	78.74%	1.35	00:00:59	1.97%	5 (7.14%)	$865.00 (9.09%)
4. 103	66 (3.06%)	63.64%	42 (2.69%)	66.67%	1.59	00:01:27	7.58%	5 (7.14%)	$715.00 (7.51%)
5. 106	73 (3.38%)	83.56%	61 (3.90%)	78.08%	1.33	00:01:15	9.59%	7 (10.00%)	$715.00 (7.51%)
6. 113	54 (2.50%)	77.78%	42 (2.69%)	64.81%	1.54	00:00:56	5.58%	3 (4.29%)	$638.00 (6.70%)
7. 119	114 (5.28%)	87.72%	100 (6.39%)	80.70%	1.35	00:01:01	3.51%	4 (5.71%)	$606.00 (6.37%)
8. 100	30 (1.39%)	83.33%	25 (1.60%)	73.33%	1.33	00:00:51	10.00%	3 (4.29%)	$407.00 (4.28%)
9. 127	22 (1.02%)	50.00%	11 (0.70%)	72.73%	1.36	00:01:00	4.55%	1 (1.43%)	$374.00 (3.93%)
10. 117	70 (3.24%)	82.86%	58 (3.71%)	67.14%	1.46	00:01:04	2.86%	2 (2.86%)	$338.00 (3.55%)
11. 102	72 (3.34%)	73.61%	53 (3.39%)	72.22%	1.79	00:02:31	4.17%	3 (4.29%)	$317.00 (3.33%)
12. 105	37 (1.71%)	45.95%	17 (1.09%)	64.86%	2.14	00:01:25	5.41%	2 (2.86%)	$283.00 (2.97%)
13. 108	144 (6.67%)	83.33%	120 (7.67%)	62.50%	1.66	00:01:39	3.47%	5 (7.14%)	$199.00 (2.09%)
14. 123	72 (3.34%)	63.89%	46 (2.94%)	70.83%	1.56	00:01:32	1.39%	1 (1.43%)	$139.00 (1.46%)
15. 115	39 (1.81%)	69.23%	27 (1.73%)	71.79%	1.36	00:01:23	2.56%	1 (1.43%)	$129.00 (1.36%)
16. 111	46 (2.13%)	82.61%	38 (2.43%)	73.91%	1.46	00:00:37	2.17%	1 (1.43%)	$119.00 (1.25%)
17. 129	31 (1.44%)	19.35%	6 (0.38%)	51.61%	2.58	00:05:55	3.23%	1 (1.43%)	$109.00 (1.15%)
18. 124	16 (0.74%)	56.25%	9 (0.58%)	68.75%	1.94	00:01:10	6.25%	1 (1.43%)	$99.00 (1.04%)

Focus on Quality over Quantity

Although cross-promotions can be a great tool, make sure you're only reaching out to campaigns you really think your community will like, and vice versa. This is really about quality over quantity. You don't want to overload your backers with projects that aren't compatible. And using irrelevant projects to promote you probably won't drive any sales.

CHAPTER

Finishing Strong

The last week of your campaign is exciting! Just like with the initial launch, you should see a higher conversion rate during this time. That's because if someone doesn't back your campaign now, they know they might miss out on the discount forever. You'll lean into this urgency with your marketing.

The two most effective channels in the final week will be your email list and Meta ads. Let's look at the email strategy first.

Final Emails

During the last week of your campaign, you'll be sending three emails to your entire email list. As with the launch email sequence, I suggest segmenting your emails by VIPs and non-VIPs, so you can craft more specific messaging for each audience. I'll go over each email from a high level.

Email 1: Three days left

Send at: 11AM EST three days before the campaign ends

- Announce the campaign's end date and time.
- Focus on the urgency to back the campaign before it ends.

Email 2: Final morning

Send at: 11AM EST on the last day

- Let your audience know that the campaign ends at midnight.
- Focus on the urgency to back the campaign before it ends.

Email 3: Final evening

Send at: 8PM EST on the last day

- Apologize for sending another email, but let them know it's the final reminder that the campaign ends at midnight.
- Focus on the urgency to back the campaign before it ends.

I've found that three emails is the perfect number. Even though your campaign will be launching on Indiegogo InDemand right when the campaign ends (and yes, you'll read more about this strongly suggested strategy shortly!), you can still lean into the fact that the "live" campaign will end at midnight and the price will go up. This is a strong motivator for people to buy.

Download our *Final Emails Template* by scanning the QR code or going to crowdfundedbook.com/email.

Meta Advertising

During the final week, you'll focus on phase 3 advertising. As with your email marketing, your ad messaging will be focused on urgency.

Next, which audiences do you target, and how can you craft the best ad? Let's see.

AUDIENCES

During phase 3 advertising, you'll focus on remarketing audiences like in phase 1. Remarketing audiences are typically the most qualified, and we've found conversion rates from these audiences are the highest during the beginning and end of a campaign.

Here are the audiences I recommend targeting:

- VIP email list
- Non-VIP email list
- Visitors who added to cart but didn't buy
- Web traffic from the campaign page that didn't purchase or add to cart

You can also try to target your best-performing audiences from phase 2, but we've found that the highest returns will come from the audiences listed above.

AD COPY AND CREATIVE

Every ad should include the same copy, making it clear that there's one last chance to take advantage of the biggest discounts before the price goes up.

Here's an example of a phase 3 ad for our campaign, AIR PIX.

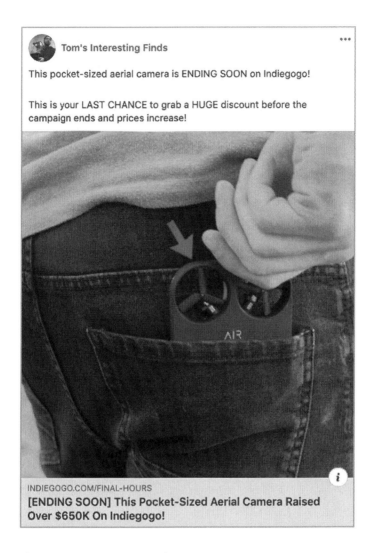

Here's the primary text we used:

This pocket-sized aerial camera is ENDING SOON on Indiegogo!

This is your LAST CHANCE to grab a HUGE discount before the campaign ends and prices increase!

Here's the headline copy we used:

ENDING SOON This Pocked-Sized Aerial Camera Raised Over $650K On Indiegogo!

In both the primary text and headline, you can see how we focused on urgency. Using words such as "ending soon" and "last chance" make it extremely clear that readers need to purchase *now* to take advantage of the discounts.

For the ad creative, I recommend using the best-performing creative from phase 1 and phase 2.

See our best-performing ads by downloading the *LaunchBoom Ad Library*. Scan the QR code or go to crowdfundedbook.com/ad-library.

More Tips

CAMPAIGN UPDATES DURING THE FINAL WEEK

I suggest sending very few campaign updates during the final week of the campaign. As a matter of fact, I wouldn't send *any*. As I mentioned earlier, we've seen a correlation between campaign updates in the final week of the campaign and backers canceling their orders. I would advise holding off on sending a campaign update until the campaign ends.

INDIEGOGO INDEMAND

If you launched on Kickstarter, you should start setting up your Indiegogo InDemand campaign during the final week of your campaign. I'll go into more detail about how to do this in the later chapter called Indiegogo InDemand. But it's good to know now that you can start to set this up before you end the campaign.

If you are on Indiegogo, your campaign will automatically change to InDemand when the campaign ends as long as you "opt in" to InDemand in the backend of your campaign.

Gearing Up for the Next Phase

You've accomplished so much already – but the next phase is where things start to become real. Once the live campaign ends, it's time to make your product a reality.

Yes, you will continue to take pre-orders through Indiegogo InDemand, but your main focus should switch to manufacturing the best product possible and getting it to your backers on time.

Before you dive into the strategies outlined in the next part of the book, take a minute to congratulate yourself. Most campaigns fail. You've joined the minority of campaigns that actually succeed!

PART 6:
POST-CAMPAIGN TACTICS

CHAPTER

What Happens if I Fail?

"Hold up here, Mark. You're talking about failing, right after you talked about having a successful campaign?"

Yes. Yes, I am.

And this isn't some tricky "tear you down after building you up" tactic.

It's actually the opposite. Understanding that "failure" may not actually be failure is empowering. And I can prove it.

Meet Simon

In April of 2022, Simon Lasnier pushed the "cancel" button on his Kickstarter campaign. After years of hard work, his campaign had failed.

Simon had created the Midronome, a synchronization device for electronic musicians.

As a musician, he built the product to solve his own problem. And it worked really well. So well, in fact, that it didn't take long for his musician friends to ask him about it.

Realizing he could make a business out of this product, he decided to launch it.

He'd already gotten so far on his own that he didn't look for any help with his Kickstarter.

And, as you already know, the campaign failed.

Meet Igor

Igor launched his first campaign on November 8, 2017. Thirty-eight days later, he pressed the cancel button. After pouring his heart and soul into his product, he had failed.

The fate of Igor's creation, the HipStar: the world's best hands-free travel cart, was uncertain, to say the least.

The idea for HipStar had come to him as he was traveling across Europe. Igor had one backpack to carry all his things, and it didn't take long for his shoulders and back to feel the weight.

Deciding to solve his own problem (just like Simon), Igor went for it on his own.

And when he launched, he only raised $10,800 of his $50,000 goal.

Failure, you might say.

They Didn't Quit, Though!

Most product creators quit after a failed campaign, but Simon and Igor were not "most" creators. Rather than viewing the events as failures, these creators saw them as an opportunity to learn.

They identified their mistakes, learned from them, and prepared to launch again.

But the next time, they decided to work with my team at LaunchBoom.

The results, you ask?

Simon relaunched and drove €159,576 in presale revenue.

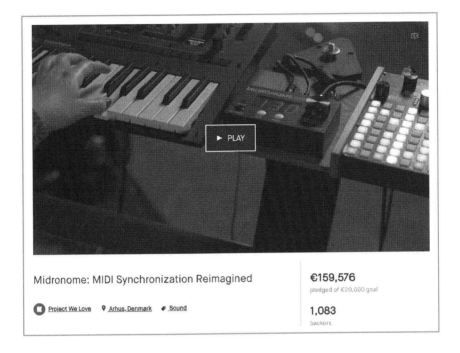

Igor relaunched and drove $102,801 in presale revenue.

Don't Make Their Mistakes

Simon and Igor were able to achieve success the second time because they didn't repeat three big mistakes.

MISTAKE #1: NOT BUILDING A BIG ENOUGH PRELAUNCH EMAIL LIST

Initially, neither of them had built a big enough prelaunch email list, so of course they weren't able to get funded on the first day. Without the momentum of a big launch, their first campaigns were practically dead in the water.

MISTAKE #2: NOT USING THE RESERVATION FUNNEL

The emails that they did have on their prelaunch list generated no reservations. That's because they didn't use a reservation funnel to build their lists. And since they hadn't gone through the reservation funnel process, their lists weren't qualified.

MISTAKE #3: THEY WENT AT IT ALONE

Bringing a product to life is *hard*. Doing it alone is even harder. Is it possible? Yes. But the likelihood of failure is dramatically increased.

I think (well, I *know*) that Simon and Igor were very happy to have help the second time.

Simon posted this in our *LaunchBoom Community* after getting funded:

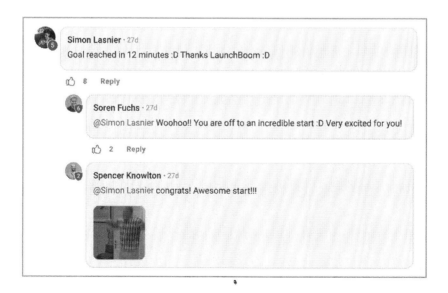

And Igor left us this review:

"LaunchBoom changed my life, seriously. I have customers from 25+ countries, and my brand has been recognized worldwide. The CBS TV Channel made a video about me and my project! LaunchBoom – thank you - I love you - and wish you great success! "

Igor Koshutin

Turning Failure into Success

Use the tips I've provided, avoid these mistakes, and you will dramatically decrease your chance of failure. But more importantly, I hope this chapter dispels any fear you have that a failed campaign is the end of the world. Because these stories prove otherwise.

CHAPTER

Getting Paid

Y ou've been working for months (maybe even years) to get to this point. Your campaign is funded, you have a community of backers, and you're ready to start making your product.

All you need now is the money. Let's talk about getting paid.

When Do You Get Paid?

On Indiegogo, your campaign funds (minus fees) will be sent to your bank account exactly fifteen days after the campaign ends.

It's also worth noting that if you raise more than 1,000 units in your currency, Indiegogo holds 5 percent of your funds in reserve, which they call "reserved funds." They hold those reserved funds for at least six months after the campaign ends.

On Kickstarter, your campaign funds (minus fees) will be sent to your bank account exactly fourteen days after the campaign ends. How

285

Kickstarter calculates the amount they send you is slightly more complicated than with Indiegogo.

FAILED CREDIT CARDS ON KICKSTARTER

On Kickstarter, a backer's credit card is not charged until the campaign ends. With potentially thousands of backers being charged at once, it's common for a portion of these credit cards to fail to charge. Reasons range from insufficient funds to overcautious application of fraud protection policies at the backer's credit institution.

Before we get into how you can reduce the number of dropped backers, let's talk about what you can expect.

Here's a breakdown of the percentage of failed credit cards in eleven campaigns we've worked on that each raised over $100K. I chose campaigns with average pledge amounts spanning a range from $47 to $526.

Percentage Failed	Average Pledge	
6.20%	$	147
4.70%	$	53
4.30%	$	95
4.20%	$	296
3.80%	$	86
3.28%	$	181
2.20%	$	152
2.13%	$	47
1.60%	$	108
1.29%	$	65
0.53%	$	526

I've heard many say that the percentage of failed credit cards usually correlates to the average pledge amount, where a higher average pledge equals a higher percentage of failed credit cards.

This sample of eleven cases does not fit that hypothesis.

What I believe affects the percentage of failed credit cards the most is *who your backers are*. For example, if your backers are primarily in a young demographic, or if there's a high percentage of backers from foreign countries, you will probably experience more failed credit cards.

Other than those thoughts, I have no formula to offer for calculating likely failed credit card percentages.

The best thing to do is to use averages. From all of our campaigns, the average failed credit card percentage is right around 3 percent. So I would recommend using 3 percent when estimating the percentage of failed credit cards you will have.

KICKSTARTER'S POST-CAMPAIGN TIMELINE

Before I get into the strategy you can apply to try to reverse the failed credit cards, let's have you see the applicable timeline after your campaign ends on Kickstarter. In order, it goes like this:

1. **Campaign ends.** Credit cards are charged. A percentage of backers become "errored" backers and per Kickstarter policies, they have one week to fix their credit card.
2. **Seven days after the end.** All errored backers become dropped backers and can no longer fix their credit card issues.
3. **Fourteen days after the end.** Money is transferred from Kickstarter to your bank account.

Now that you understand the timeline, here's the best strategy to reverse failed credit cards.

SEND PERSONAL MESSAGES

When a backer's credit card fails, Kickstarter sends them a notification asking them to fix the issue within seven days. This is useful, but you can also take matters into your own hands and deal with your errored backers directly.

After your campaign ends, go to your Backer Report. In the "All backers" dropdown, you can choose your "Errored backers."

Then select all backers with failed credit cards. You then have the option to message just those backers – directly, and all at once.

We like to send two messages to errored backers during this time. The first message is sent right after your campaign ends and looks like this:

Hey there,

I noticed that your credit card failed to charge for your [product] pre-order! I wanted to personally reach out to let you know that you only have 1 week to fix it on Kickstarter. If you don't, then I can't guarantee that you'll get your [product] at your Kickstarter discount.

Please let me know if you have any questions!

-[your name]

The second message should be sent six days after the campaign ends, and would look like this:

Hey there,

Hope all is well! I just want to remind you that this is the *last chance* to update your credit information on Kickstarter. If you don't, then I can't guarantee that you'll get your [product] at the discounted price.

Please login to Kickstarter and correct your credit card information as soon as you can.

If you don't by tomorrow, you will be dropped as a Kickstarter backer!

Please let me know if you have any questions!

-[your name]

This strategy usually saves about 20–30 percent of errored backers from becoming dropped backers.

Using This Information

Use this information to budget for how many payments will likely fail at the end of your campaign. Losing a small percentage of backers may seem negligible, but it adds up, along with all the other fees taken by Kickstarter and any other services you use.

More importantly, know that you can do something about failed credit card payments. Reach out personally to your backers so you get your funds, and they get the product they tried to back in the first place.

CHAPTER

Indiegogo InDemand

Once your live campaign ends, the party's not over. Indiegogo InDemand keeps it going long into the night. That's because Indiegogo InDemand allows you to continue pre-selling after your Kickstarter or Indiegogo campaign ends.

That's right. Think of it like a pre-order store that can be up indefinitely.

One of the coolest parts about InDemand is that even if you launched on Kickstarter, Indiegogo will start your InDemand campaign by including the funding amount from your live campaign.

For example, our campaign for LoftTek raised $757,079 on Kickstarter.

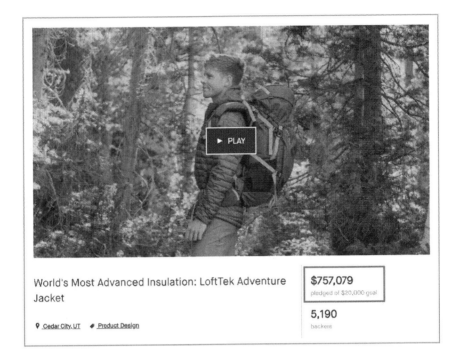

World's Most Advanced Insulation: LoftTek Adventure Jacket

$757,079
pledged of $20,000 goal

5,190
backers

♀ Cedar City, UT ✎ Product Design

Immediately after we finished on Kickstarter, we transferred over to Indiegogo InDemand.

On InDemand, we started at $757,079 — the final amount raised on Kickstarter. We then went on to raise a grand total of $1,041,308 in presale revenue after the campaign ran its course on InDemand.

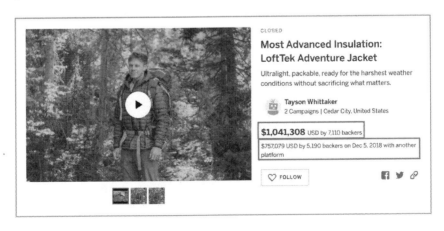

CLOSED

Most Advanced Insulation: LoftTek Adventure Jacket

Ultralight, packable, ready for the harshest weather conditions without sacrificing what matters.

Tayson Whittaker
2 Campaigns | Cedar City, United States

$1,041,308 USD by 7,110 backers

$757,079 USD by 5,190 backers on Dec 5, 2018 with another platform

♡ FOLLOW

To me, using Indiegogo InDemand is a no-brainer. Let me show you how to set it up.

Getting Set Up on InDemand

INDIEGOGO SETUP

Let's get the easy one out of the way first. To convert your campaign to InDemand if you launched on Indiegogo, simply "opt-in" to InDemand in the backend of your campaign.

As of the date of writing this book, there is a section within the Indiegogo campaign editor called InDemand. Just check the box that says you want to go to InDemand and you'll be set. Once the funding duration ends, the campaign will automatically transfer to InDemand.

KICKSTARTER SETUP

If you launched first on Kickstarter, you can still launch on InDemand. I suggest getting your InDemand campaign set up during the final week of your Kickstarter campaign.

To get started, go to Indiegogo.com and proceed the same way you would if you were setting up a campaign from scratch. Once your campaign is complete in draft mode, reach out to indemand@indiegogo.com with a link to your Kickstarter campaign. They'll approve you and switch your campaign so it's eligible for InDemand.

The second after your Kickstarter campaign ends, you can launch your Indiegogo InDemand campaign. The record of the funds raised on Kickstarter will be automatically pulled into your InDemand campaign.

After you've launched on InDemand, you should set up your Kickstarter Spotlight page. Refreshing your Kickstarter campaign page after the campaign finishes takes you to the Kickstarter Spotlight setup.

You can add a button to your Kickstarter Spotlight page that links it to your Indiegogo InDemand campaign. That way, any traffic that continues to go to your Kickstarter page can be redirected to your InDemand campaign.

COSTS AND PAYOUTS

If you launched on Indiegogo first, Indiegogo InDemand takes a 5 percent fee, just like your live campaign.

If you launched on Kickstarter first, Indiegogo InDemand takes an 8 percent fee. Indiegogo uses an increased fee to disincentivize creators from launching on Kickstarter first. Kickstarter creators typically aren't too happy about this, but I recommend using Indiegogo InDemand anyway.

Payouts are made roughly every four weeks and can be tracked within the Indiegogo backend.

Driving Sales through InDemand

In my experience, the largest sources of revenue to an InDemand campaign are Meta advertising and Indiegogo's promotions, especially their newsletter. The sales we drive from Meta advertising unlock Indiegogo promotions, which, in turn, drive more sales.

When you get on InDemand, ask an Indiegogo representative what funding amount you need to reach to unlock newsletter placement. Whatever number they tell you will be your next funding goal, and you can use Meta advertising to hit it.

Once you do hit it, you can see how lucrative an Indiegogo newsletter is for your campaign. In my experience, it drives at minimum a few thousand dollars to the campaign. I've also seen a single newsletter drive as much as $40K.

Repeat the cycle. Ask for a new funding threshold to unlock newsletter placement and make that your goal. Since you've already seen the effectiveness of one newsletter, you have an idea of how much another spot in their newsletter is worth to you.

Be aware, though: You should expect the next newsletter to perform 15-30 percent worse than the previous one. That knowledge can help you evaluate the acceptable ROAS for InDemand.

As an example, let's say that a single Indiegogo newsletter will send roughly $20K in sales. You could accept a lower return on ad spend, knowing that there will be a $20K increase in sales once you reach the funding threshold.

Shutting InDemand Down

I recommend continuing to sell on InDemand until you have inventory and are ready to sell on your e-commerce website. Once you know the day you'll go live with your e-commerce website, you should reach out to the Indiegogo team and inform them of the last day of your InDemand campaign. Request that they put a countdown timer on the campaign to increase urgency for any final visitors.

CHAPTER

Pledge Management

Pledge management: As a concept unique to crowdfunding, it's probably within this book that you heard those two words together for the first time. But once your crowdfunding campaign is over, you'll be hearing the words "pledge management" *a lot*.

A pledge manager is a software tool that allows you to manage the key backer information required for fulfillment. It will collect and confirm:

- Shipping information
- Add-on and upsell information
- Product variant information (sizes, colors, etc.)

Both Kickstarter and Indiegogo collect some of that information while a backer is finishing their order. But since you won't be shipping your product for some time after the campaign ends, it's important to re-confirm all this information, and also request some additional information.

Which Pledge Manager Should You Use?

The two categories of pledge managers are "third-party" and "native." Third-party options are separate and apart from the crowdfunding platform, and exist to make the pledge management process easier (and also have added functionality). Native options are pledge management tools that exist within the crowdfunding platforms.

NATIVE OPTIONS

Kickstarter has a basic built-in pledge manager. After your campaign ends, you can create surveys that can be customized based on the backer's reward level. Surveys enable you to collect product variant information (size, color, etc.) and the backer's shipping address. It's pretty basic, but it works, and it's free.

On Indiegogo, pledge management is a little different. They don't have surveys like Kickstarter, because Indiegogo asks for shipping and product variant information while a backer is checking out. You can, however, add tracking numbers and manage everything from Indiegogo's backend.

Both Kickstarter and Indiegogo have integrations with EasyShip, which is pretty awesome because you can export your backer information and upload directly to EasyShip. Of course, that's only is a useful feature if you plan to use EasyShip for fulfillment. If you're not sure who you'll use, I recommend you check out EasyShip.

THIRD-PARTY

There really aren't many companies in the third-party pledge management space. The two our clients work with the most are BackerKit and PledgeBox. BackerKit came first and is the most experienced. PledgeBox is essentially a copycat (but a very good one) and generally more affordable than BackerKit.

One to watch will be PledgeManager.com. As of the date of this writing, Kickstarter just announced an official partnership with them. There is very little information currently available, but by the time you're reading this, there may be much more! I recommend checking them out and comparing them to BackerKit and PledgeBox.

The main value of third-party pledge managers is the additional features they offer over native options. I like to think of them as a platform to manage your entire post-campaign fulfillment process.

Just like with native options, you can collect shipping and product variant information. Other very effective features such as advanced shipping information collection and my favorite, upselling, are available, too.

Upselling, all on its own, usually makes a third-party option worth it. Very rarely does a client not make back their pledge manager investment from the upsell feature alone…but more on that to come in just a bit.

To date, we've seen more clients gravitating to PledgeBox. For that reason, I'm going to dive into how we use PledgeBox during the post-campaign, but understand that much of the strategy applies equally to any third-party pledge manager.

You can sign up for your PledgeBox account by scanning the QR code or going to crowdfundedbook.com/pledgebox.

Using a Third-Party Pledge Manager

SETUP

When your Kickstarter or Indiegogo campaign ends, you can start to set up your PledgeBox account. Once that's done, PledgeBox will walk you through a simple setup process to get you ready to send your surveys.

You'll start by using their integration to import your backers into their platform. This way, all the backer's information (name, email, product backed, etc.) will be brought in to save you time later.

Don't be afraid to reach out to the PledgeBox team if you get stuck. They have great support and will be happy to help you through it.

UPSELLS

One of the primary reasons we recommend PledgeBox is its upsell capability: After your backers have filled out your survey and provided any product variant information, they are taken to a page with more products they can buy. You can configure which products you want to appear on the page before you go live with your survey.

Our campaign for The Empire sunglasses by William Painter is a good example. Since they had already sold many other styles of sunglasses on their site, we added all of those items as upsells.

We were able to sell an additional $40,768 in product *just from those upsells*. This more than covered the cost of using a third-party pledge manager and helped William Painter dramatically increase their average order value.

But what if you don't have additional products to upsell? Then just upsell additional units of your main product. I just want to make sure you know that every time we've added even just one item as an upsell, we've driven more sales.

FULFILLMENT

Once you're ready to fulfill, PledgeBox will make it a breeze. They have direct integrations with many of the top fulfillment companies. If you want to do something custom, you can download the CSV files yourself. Once you start shipping, you can add tracking numbers to PledgeBox so all backers can track their shipments themselves.

The Best Choice for Most Campaigns

Even though it's not absolutely necessary to use a third-party pledge manager for your campaign, I think that their features make it an easy choice for most. Just by using the upsell tool, most campaigners are able to more than cover the cost of using the service.

Moreover, the upsell tool is just one of many powerful features a pledge manager offers. You should at last explore using a third-party pledge manager. Very rarely will it not be worth it.

PART 7:
BUILDING A LONG-TERM BRAND

CHAPTER

The Power of Long-Term Thinking

"So, how much are you looking to raise with your crowdfunding campaign?" I ask.

"A million dollars, at a minimum," Jim, the potential client, replies.

"Okay, great. Why that much?" I ask.

"Well, I saw that Coolest Cooler raised $13 million, and my product is way better. So if we don't raise a million, I'm going to consider it a failure."

I probe a little. "So just to be clear, if you raised $999,999, your campaign would be a failure?"

Now looking a little unsure of himself, Jim answers, "Um… yes, that's right. We'd need to hit a million dollars."

Interactions like this are incredibly common, in my experience — creators fixated on making over $1 million because they somehow have the idea that it signifies success. I've come to realize that often, this fixation on short-term success is fueled by ego, when a more useful perspective would be focusing on long-term business success, fueled by vision.

But I get it.

At LaunchBoom, we are often judged by the number of dollars we've raised for our clients, not how successful our clients are over the long term.

Few know that 0.12 percent of campaigns ever reach $1 million. Or that the Coolest Cooler that raised $13M on Kickstarter had to sell on Amazon to "keep the lights on" before even shipping to Kickstarter backers. Or that Pebble, one of the most funded Kickstarter campaigns ever, had to sell all its assets to Fitbit three months after its latest multi-million-dollar campaign ended.

Since LaunchBoom began in 2015, I've come to realize that raising $1 million on Indiegogo or Kickstarter isn't the most important factor to focus on. That's because **short-term crowdfunding success does not equal long-term business success.**

You may be wondering why I'm talking about this near the end of the book. It's simple: Now that you understand how campaigns are able to raise $1M+, you must understand that it's usually *not* that important.

Unless you're looking to close up shop after you ship product to your crowdfunding backers, your campaign is destined to be just a tiny blip in your company's existence. In many respects, it's going to be one of the smoothest periods of your company's existence. Once you actually have to fulfill your product, the hard part begins.

With all this said, the short-term goal of a large crowdfunding campaign is not inherently bad. There are many successful businesses that started with a $1M+ campaign. But it's important to be aware of the reasons you feel that $1M+ campaign is necessary for you to achieve your business goals. If the reason is that you believe a huge crowdfunding raise is absolutely necessary for you to achieve long-term business success, you should probably find a different reason.

It might be helpful to take a look at common myths around the importance of a large crowdfunding raise, and then some unique challenges that often arise with large crowdfunding campaigns. My goal is to give you more clarity on how crowdfunding aligns with your long-term business goals.

Myths about Large Crowdfunding Campaigns

MYTH #1: INVESTORS ARE MOST INTERESTED IN LARGE CAMPAIGNS

Many creators plan to raise investment capital post-crowdfunding, and believe that having a large campaign raise is critical to attracting investor interest. While it is true that having a large campaign does make your company more interesting to potential investors, it is *not* the most important thing.

I reached out to serial crowdfunder and client, Kevin Liang, to weigh in on the subject. He has not only raised more than $1.5M across his product launches, but he's also raised investment capital, many times, post-crowdfunding. Here's what he had to say:

"Investors now know that a large crowdfunding campaign does not equate to post crowdfunding success. More sophisticated investors are now more interested in learning about the fulfillment, defect rate, customer loyalty, etc. from delivering the crowdfunding campaign."

Kevin Liang I CEO & Founder
Raised $1.5M+ through crowdfunding
Ecoqube

In other words, sophisticated investors are more interested in other metrics that are better predictors of long-term success. It makes sense, since they are going to be betting on your company being more valuable in the long term.

What would happen if instead of being so fixated on the number of dollars raised, you focused on being able to fulfill on time, the quality of the product, or providing the best experience backers will ever have with a brand? You'd then be focusing on metrics more correlated with long-term business success. I think we'd see a healthier crowdfunding ecosystem, as well as more successful businesses.

MYTH #2: RETAILERS AND DISTRIBUTORS ARE MOST INTERESTED IN LARGE CAMPAIGNS

Just like the myth around what's most important to investors, many entrepreneurs believe having a large raise is most important for retailers as well.

I asked Greg Appelhof, President and CEO of SPRING (a strategic retail accelerator), to weigh in on the subject. Here's what he had to say:

Although Retail initially got excited about the prospects of crowdfunding— the euphoria quickly dissolved.

Today, crowdfunding is an important market marker, with crowdfunding being an amazing tool to understand product/market fit, customer profile, product preference and roadmap. When crowdfunding is followed by timely shipment, great product reviews, operational and manufacturing scale, and a roadmap beyond the "Hit" product, then Retail can gain confidence in a company who uses crowdfunding as a product launch strategy. Retailers do not create categories, entrepreneurs and innovation companies do. Crowdfunding has accelerated this process across many categories. Retail has benefitted from this new channel of innovation.

What crowdfunding does best is bring AMAZING global recognition. Retailers use this as a gauge and then look for evidence the company can execute.

Greg Appelhof I CEO & President
Strategic Retail Accelerator
SPRING

Again, the myth surrounding retailers is similar to the investment myth. While retailers gauge interest in a product by how well the crowdfunding campaign did, it's not the most important metric. They are more interested in your ability to execute. That includes delivering a high-quality product on time, delivering a great customer experience, and being able to scale manufacturing and fulfillment to meet demand.

MYTH #3: I NEED TO RAISE ALL THE FUNDS BEFORE MY INDIEGOGO OR KICKSTARTER CAMPAIGN ENDS

Since the beginning of crowdfunding, campaigns have been structured with a start and end date — anywhere between one and sixty days long, on both Kickstarter and Indiegogo. Many creators are fixated on raising large amounts during their campaign duration, and in too many cases, at all costs.

Years ago, however, Indiegogo's added feature, InDemand, made this much less important. As you've learned, InDemand makes it easy to keep selling after your live campaign is over. For example, our client SPRYNG raised $601,927 on Kickstarter and then raised an additional $473,855 on InDemand — bringing the total to $1,075,782 raised.

Challenges of Large Campaigns

CHALLENGE #1: NOT HAVING ENOUGH MARGIN

It's difficult to have a highly profitable campaign that also raises over 1 million dollars. Why? Because running a large campaign costs money, and a lot of it.

Right from the start, there's about a 10 percent haircut from the crowdfunding platform, as well as payment processing fees. If you work with a crowdfunding agency, there's a commission on funds raised (let's say, 10 percent), so now you're at 20 percent right off the top. Further, in your crowdfunding campaign, it's a best practice to heavily discount your product, since backers are technically pre-ordering. The amount you discount varies, but the point is, that's more margin taken out.

Next, there are the costs of setting up the campaign: video production, graphic design, PR, etc. And you'll spend money on digital ads, where returns can vary widely. But just for the sake of simplicity, let's say you get a 3x return on ad spend. To have a positive gross margin, you'll need to have at least 33 percent left in your margin after all the other costs mentioned above.

Simply put, margins are *tight* on large campaigns. If you aren't careful with your spending on crowdfunding, you can easily be very unprofitable. Unless you have extra cash set aside, not having gross profit means you won't have money to actually make the product you're crowdfunding for.

This is exactly what happened to the Coolest Cooler campaign that raised $13M but then needed to continue to sell on Amazon to "keep the lights on."

CHALLENGE #2: NOT BEING ABLE TO FULFILL ORDERS ON TIME

I've seen creators raise large amounts of money, but then have no idea how the correspondingly large numbers of orders would affect manufacturing and fulfillment timelines. Manufacturers can't magically produce any number of your products at the same time.

That goes for fulfillment, too. You're not staffed like Amazon, with always enough people to physically pick, pack, and ship every order every day. The more orders you get, the more time it can take for manufacturing and fulfillment.

If you plan to have a large raise, it's important to know how much volume your manufacturer can handle and how quickly you can fulfill those orders. Use this information to batch your perks and rewards by different estimated delivery dates.

For example, you can have batch one ship three months from now, and plan to have batch two ship four months from now. This more doable timeline will be more accurate, helping you to manage the expectations of your backers.

CHALLENGE #3: NOT MAKING A HIGH-QUALITY PRODUCT

On the flip side of not fulfilling on time, I've seen creators rush their products to meet delivery time, only to deliver a low-quality product. Very sadly, because they were so inundated with orders from their large campaign raise, they became more focused on the additional work that came from the financial windfall. Instead, they should have been focused on creating the product they promised backers and delivering an amazing customer experience.

What's the Definition of Success?

I was interviewing Callan, one of our clients. When I asked him what his definition of success was, he said, "If I'm able to continue to e-commerce and scale my business, my crowdfunding campaign was a success."

Interesting, I thought. His answer seemed close to the truth.

Success, whether in crowdfunding or elsewhere, means **you are setting yourself up best for whatever comes next.**

With the Coolest Cooler, raising $13 million seemed "successful," but it didn't set the brand up for what would come next: e-commerce. Instead, the creators scrambled for five years to fulfill the orders, facing challenge after challenge because they had raised so much.

On the other hand, one client who raised $50K on crowdfunding had an extremely strong foundation for e-commerce. Eight months after we started working with them, we had already hit seven figures in revenue. Ten months after that, we hit eight figures.

After more thought about Callan's response, I asked myself, "What must be true to best set up a product creator for e-commerce success?"

My Definition of Success

I'll admit, I wish the answer to success was as easy as saying "You need to raise X number of dollars on your crowdfunding campaign." But life isn't always easy, and neither are answers :) Instead, the answer is multi-dimensional.

To me, finally, it comes down to (1) achieving very specific goals, and (2) having a thorough understanding of your business's key aspects. Here are all the things I believe must be true for a campaign to be successful.

1) You achieve three goals.

- You acquire customers profitably and thereby validate you have a market.
- You pay for your first manufacturing run.
- You ship your product on time (or close to on time).

2) You understand specific key aspects of your business.

- Business metrics
  - Cost to produce your product
  - Cost to ship your product
  - Cost to acquire a customer

- Who your customers are and what they respond to
  - Which audiences are most likely to buy your product
  - Which product messaging resonates the most with those audiences
  - Which customer acquisition channels are most effective

Accomplishing the goals above and ending the campaign with an understanding of your core business isn't easy, but it's necessary. That will put you in a much better position to move to e-commerce and begin to scale.

Long- (Not Short-) Term Profitability Is the Goal

I want to zoom in on profitability for a moment, so you don't misunderstand me. I did *not* say that your goal is to be profitable on the campaign. I said your goal is to acquire customers profitably. The difference is important.

With a crowdfunding campaign (or any product launch), there are many costs to get it off the ground. Because of that, very few campaigns make a profit. The ones that do are typically repeat crowdfunders, because they can leverage past success to lower their marketing costs.

When you play a long-term game, profitability on the crowdfund is not the goal – instead, proving you can acquire a customer profitably is. If you do that, you are much more likely to build a scalable e-commerce business post-crowdfunding.

How to Use This Information

Whether you use my definition or not, take the time to think about what success means to you before you launch your campaign. More importantly, take the time to understand why you're defining success the way you are, and how it will set you up to transition to e-commerce. Doing this work up front will force you to focus on what's most important to your long-term business success.

CHAPTER

Bonus: Transitioning to E-Commerce

E-commerce is the final phase of our journey. Once you've manufactured your product, shipped to your backers, and have inventory to sell on your e-commerce website, you can capitalize on the success of your crowdfunding campaign and begin to scale.

Remember the product adoption curve that I talked about earlier in the book? Here's a refresher:

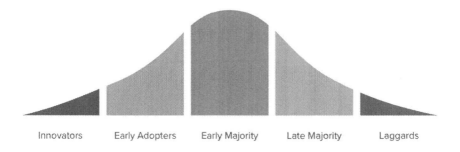

Innovators   Early Adopters   Early Majority   Late Majority   Laggards

Up until this point, you've been capturing customers from the innovators and early adopters segments. As you transition to e-commerce, you'll be opening yourself up to the mass market. Which means you'll have even more potential customers to sell to.

Plus, now that you have literal "buy-in" from the innovators and early adopters, the mass market will be more likely to buy your product.

Simply put, there's a lot to be excited about with this transition!

Let's start with how to build your e-commerce website.

Building Your E-Commerce Website

I would recommend building your site using Shopify. It's awesome… which is why it's become the most popular e-commerce platform. As of 2023, over 4.5 million sites use Shopify to power their e-commerce stores.

You can get a free trial by scanning the QR code or going to crowdfundedbook.com/shopify.

THEMES

Besides being fully customizable, Shopify also has "themes" you can use to get off the ground quickly. These themes come in two shapes and sizes, free and paid. As you probably guessed, the paid themes are better, with more functionality and better design. Best part is, at only a few hundred dollars, they are super affordable.

I recommend going with a paid theme. You can try one out before you have to make a decision, and you only have to pay for it once you decide to use it on your main site.

APPS

If you want to extend the functionality of your store, Shopify has an entire app marketplace, with lots of free and paid apps.

Want to add reviews? Want to add pop-up email capture? Want to add upsells and cross-sell functionality?

There's an app for all of those and more. By being able to easily extend the functionality of your store with an app, you can save thousands of dollars on hiring a developer.

WHEN TO BUILD YOUR SITE

I wouldn't worry about creating your e-commerce website until you've reached the stage of using Indiegogo InDemand. We typically start building our clients' e-commerce sites two months before we plan to end the InDemand campaign. (As noted earlier, the end of the InDemand campaign should be determined by when you'll have inventory to sell through e-commerce.)

DO NOT USE YOUR SITE FOR PRE-ORDERS

Many creators are tempted to take their campaigns down from Indiegogo InDemand and offer pre-orders on their own e-commerce sites. Don't you do that.

We've tested advertisements for pre-orders on clients' websites versus their InDemand campaigns. In every situation, we've found that the InDemand campaign leads to a higher return on ad spend. Why? Because consumers expect products on Indiegogo to be pre-orders. Conversely, consumers expect products on e-commerce sites to ship right away.

I recommend that you keep your pre-orders on the crowdfunding site, and only shut down your campaign when you have inventory for e-commerce.

ENDING YOUR INDEMAND CAMPAIGN

When you know when you'll have inventory for your e-commerce site, you should set a date for the end of your InDemand campaign. To make that happen, you'll have to email the Indiegogo team. I recommend including the following in your email:

1. **End date:** Tell them the exact date you want to end.
2. **Countdown timer:** Ask them to add a countdown timer to the campaign page that matches the end date of your campaign. They will often do this for you.
3. **Final promotion:** Ask if you can receive any final newsletter promotions before the campaign ends.

If you're running ads for your campaign, remember to schedule them to end when your campaign ends!

E-Commerce Marketing Strategy

Because of the success of your crowdfunding campaign, you should be able to start scaling immediately. By then, you'll have *tons* of data and understanding of what works with your marketing. You should know which audiences to target. You should know which ad creative to use. You don't have to reinvent the wheel once you get to e-commerce. Use everything you learned, and start scaling.

For example, we took a client (who requested anonymity) from a $50K Kickstarter campaign to over $5 million in the first eight months. That was because we were able to build on what we learned from the crowd-funding campaign.

Here's a screenshot of Shopify's dashboard for that client from April 1 to December 31, 2020.

We continued to work with that client for over two years and generated $21,737,166.04 in revenue, as you can see in the screenshot below.

Read on for the principles of our marketing strategy that allowed us to drive this kind of revenue for this client, and many more just like them.

Build Your Website Like a Funnel

Think about your e-commerce website as a funnel. Each page of your site should be focused on getting the visitor to take one action. Remember how simple your reservation funnel was? Emulate that simplicity for your e-commerce website and you'll have more success.

Here's an example of the e-commerce website we built for MÄNNKITCHEN.

First, you land on the home page.

If you click "SHOP NOW," you're taken to the product page of the most popular product.

From there, when the visitor clicks "ADD TO CART," they are taken to the cart.

The cart is simple but the customer will see some add-ons below the CHECK OUT button.

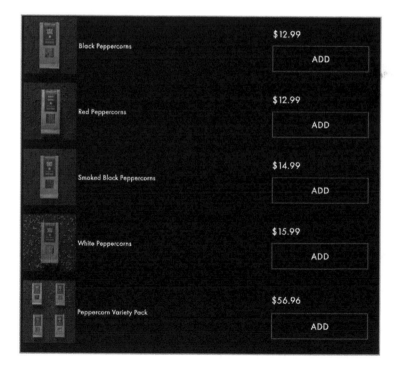

That makes it easy for visitors to add complementary products to their cart. When they're done, they click "CHECK OUT" and are taken to the Shopify default checkout. (Don't be concerned about not having much control over Shopify's checkout; it works extremely well.)

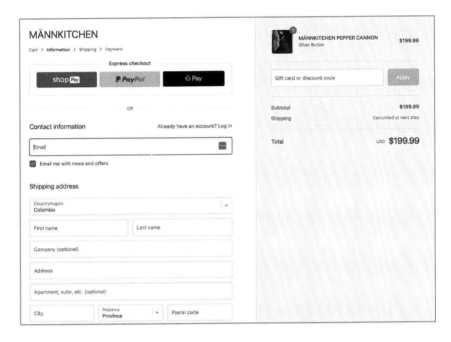

Once someone fills in their payment details, the order is done.

As you can see, we designed the e-commerce website to flow like a funnel. Within the first year of being live on Shopify, we drove $3,760,615.60 in revenue for MÄNNKITCHEN (see the screenshot below). I recommend you build your website similarly.

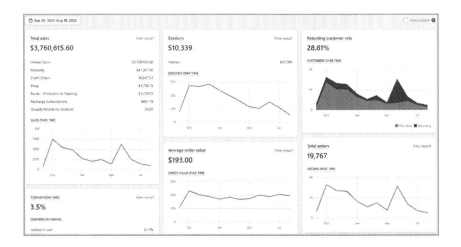

Set Up "Must-Have" Email Flows

Just like email marketing is key to the success of your launch, it will continue to be key to the success of your e-commerce business. One terrific thing here is that a huge part of your email strategy with e-commerce will be automated. I'm going to zero in on those automations next.

All the client examples that follow use email marketing software called Klaviyo. It's incredibly good and we've used it for all of our clients since 2018.

To satisfy your curiosity (or your doubt!), you can try it for free by scanning the QR code or going to crowdfundedbook.com/klaviyo.

There are three "must-have" email flows that you need to set up.

FLOW #1: WELCOME

The "welcome" flow usually drives the most sales. Offering a discount is the most typical way to get someone on your list and into this flow.

For example, look at the pop-up on MÄNNKITCHEN's website.

Once someone provides their email address, they're automatically added to the welcome flow we set up in Klaviyo.

Every automation needs a trigger to start it. In the case of the welcome flow, I recommend creating a list within Klaviyo (and call it "welcome flow"). When someone is added to that list, the flow is triggered.

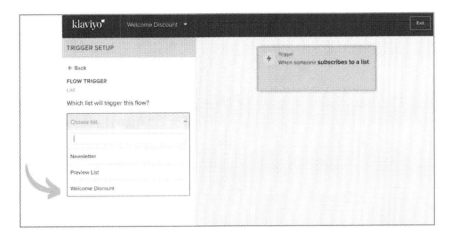

Like I said before, the most common welcome email flow is around a discount. If that's what you're going to use, then I would set up these emails:

- **Email 1**
  -) *When to send:* Immediately
  -) *What to focus on:* Keep it simple and offer the discount code

- **Email 2**
  -) *When to send:* Wait three days after email 1
  -) *What to focus on:* One to three key product benefits, and give the discount code again

- **Email 3**
  -) *When to send:* Wait four days after email 2
  -) *What to focus on:* Focus on urgency and say that the discount will run out at midnight

FLOW #2: CART ABANDONMENT

The cart abandonment flow will trigger when someone gets to checkout but does not complete their order. This can all be handled automatically within Klaviyo.

For the trigger, choose "Checkout Started."

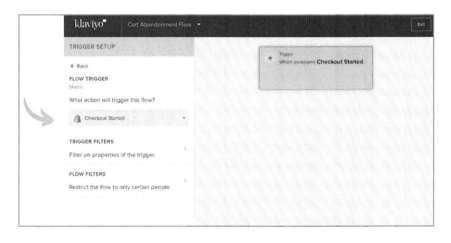

I recommend setting up two emails for that flow.

- **Email 1**
  - ○ *When to send:* Wait 4 hours
  - ○ *What to focus on:* Keep it simple and remind them that they forgot something in their cart

- **Email 2**
  - ○ *When to send:* Wait 2 days after email 1
  - ○ *What to focus on:* Offer a discount that's larger than the one you gave for the welcome discount

FLOW #3: NEW CUSTOMER

The new customer flow will trigger when someone makes a first-time purchase on your site. Unless you have lots of items to upsell, this is typically less sales-focused.

For the trigger, choose "Placed Order."

For sites with only a few products, like yours probably will be, I recommend setting up two emails.

- **Email 1**
  - ○ *When to send:* Wait 2 days
  - ○ *What to focus on:* Any instructions (including a video or PDF) that will help customers quickly understand how to use the product

▪ **Email 2**
> *When to send:* Wait 15 days after email 1
> *What to focus on:* Ask for a review

SET UP FLOW FILTERS

I also recommend setting up a "flow filter." The one I recommend setting up on almost all of your flows is shown below.

A flow filter removes someone from the flow if they place an order. This is helpful in any flow where you're trying to sell something because once someone buys, you don't want to annoy them with emails asking them to purchase.

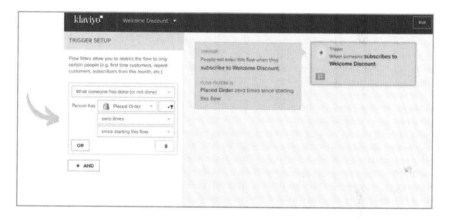

Drive Traffic with Advertising

Once you get to e-commerce, you start to expand your advertising into different channels. Still, though, Meta advertising will likely be the largest channel for most creators. It's the channel that continues to make up the majority of ad spend for our e-commerce clients. So that's why I'll focus on Meta here.

AUDIENCE TARGETING

Target your best-performing interest audiences from your crowdfunding campaign. The only major difference is to remove any "crowdfunding" narrowing you may have applied to the audiences. Remember, you're going after the mass market now.

I also suggest that you create a lookalike audience from your backer list. You will then have a new audience based on the interest and demographic profiles of your customers. Take note, though – the lookalike audience won't work very well unless you have at least 500 backers, and ideally more than 1,000.

AD CREATIVE

When you first switch to e-commerce, use your campaign's best-performing ad creative. Just remove any copy related to crowdfunding and your launch, and you'll be good.

For example, look at what we did with our client The Scoop. We first launched on Indiegogo and drove $256,806 in presale revenue. Here are screenshots of our best-performing ads.

When we transitioned to e-commerce, we changed some of the copy, but we used the same exact ad creative. Here's the ad on e-commerce.

If you have the resources to create more ads, by all means, do! But you should also be using what you know already works. You'll save time and money.

Remember the Test, Launch, Scale Framework

Of course you remember the framework I talked about at the beginning of the book… "Test, launch, scale."

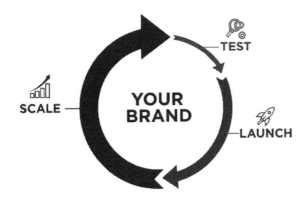

Don't forget this model. This is a cyclical, repeatable framework. Once you get to e-commerce, you can start to think about the next products you want to test. Once you've tested and found your winner, you can launch that product through crowdfunding. Once you've had a successful launch, you can add that product to your e-commerce website and continue to scale.

Then you can repeat this cycle again and again. And as it repeats, you build your brand and your community of customers — which only makes each cycle more effective.

NOW WHAT?
IMPLEMENT!

CHAPTER

Your Execution Plan

I hope you're feeling inspired, informed, and excited to launch your product. If you use what you learned here, you'll have a successful product launch within the next twelve months.

Think about that.

Within a year, your product will be launched, funded, and sold to real customers around the world. How does that make you feel?

One of the important frameworks I introduced you to would be the seven milestones to launching your product.

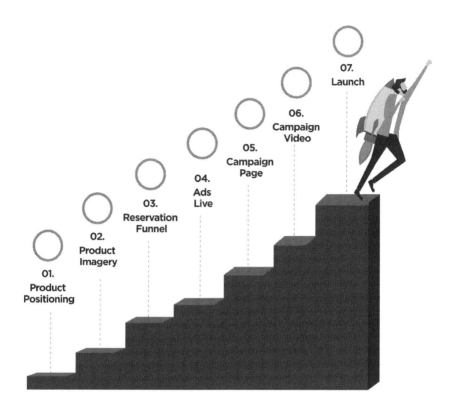

Critical here is getting your reservation funnel built and your ads live as quickly as possible. Remember, you can get this set up by using our LaunchKit software.

Learn more at <u>crowdfundedbook.com/launchkit</u>.

Once you turn on your ads and get your first email sign-ups on your reservation funnel, things start to feel real. That will give you the momentum you need to make it all the way to your launch.

After teaching you how to launch your product, I walked you through how to keep momentum up and boost your campaign.

Lastly, we talked about what comes after the campaign, including the transition to e-commerce – where you will use your launch as a springboard to scale.

"HOW'S YOUR FORM?"

A few years ago, I started to get back into weight lifting. When a new gym opened up close to my home in San Diego, I took it as the perfect sign I should start again.

I was so excited.

I mentioned to my friend, Jack, that I planned to get "ripped."

"How's your form?" he asked me.

"Pretty good, I think. I've watched a lot of YouTube videos, so I think I'll be okay."

But Jack was worried. He told me how when he first started weight lifting, he went at it alone. Everything was going along fine – until he got hurt.

So Jack found a trainer. Luke was pretty expensive, but he taught Jack what Jack needed to know – proper form. Jack said he wished he had worked with Luke from the start.

"Interesting. Can I have his number?" I asked Jack… even though, in the back of my mind, I knew I wasn't going to call.

I started hitting the gym, and everything was going well. But just a few weeks in, I got hurt doing squats.

In that instant, I knew something was off with my form, although I wasn't sure what. I remembered Jack telling me about his trainer, who ultimately made all the difference. I decided to give Luke a call.

Reluctantly, I reached out to Jack again and asked for the phone number I had lost. He responded with an "I told you so" chuckle at first, but then happily provided the number.

A week later, after sending the trainer $700, I was in my first session. Still a little skeptical. But within ten minutes, Luke pointed out more than twenty small nuances that were off.

When I made the changes, I found I could barely lift the weights. I had to relearn to lift the right way. I certainly had never realized that so many seemingly minor things could ever have made such a difference. If only I had listened to Jack and seen the trainer at the start, I would have saved so much time, money, and pain (literally).

HOW TO GET STARTED

Right now, you're probably like I was: motivated to take action on your own. But I'm like Jack was: asking you, "How's your form?"

I've seen the path in front of you, I know the problems and obstacles you'll face, and I understand how much of a difference it makes to get help.

The most common question I get asked at this point is, "Can you just help me use what you taught in this book – and can you do some of it for me?"

The answer is, yes. That's why I created LaunchBoom.

LaunchBoom is a team of experts that help product creators bring their ideas to life. From launch to manufacturing to e-commerce, we are here to help you through the entire journey of building your e-commerce business.

Our goal is to help you *finally* get off the sidelines and launch that product idea you've always had – while saving you thousands of dollars and hundreds of hours.

If launching your product is a priority, and you're serious about investing time, money, and energy into making it a success, the best first step is to book a call with my team to see how we can help you bring this all together.

On the call, we'll talk through your goals and challenges. If we look like a good fit, we'll show you how the LaunchBoom system can help you.

Full disclosure: We're *very* picky about who we work with. We get hundreds of creators every month who want to launch products with us, but we only accept about 10 percent of the applications. I'm not saying this to scare you away – I just want to manage expectations. I want you to know we only work with people we believe we can *really* help. If we don't think you're a good fit, we'll tell you – and then we'll point you in the right direction!

So if you're ready to get started, go ahead and book a call with my team at crowdfundedbook.com/call (or scan the QR code).

You've got a lot here – everything I could offer you between book covers. But what this book can't do is have a conversation with you, hold you accountable, and personalize a plan to bring your product idea to life.

Book a call now. Check your form. And start your journey right.

READY TO COMMIT TO YOUR LAUNCH?

If you're still reading, I know two things about you. First, your launch is important to you. If it weren't, you wouldn't have purchased this book and read it all the way to the end.

Second, you're committed. Most people don't finish books. By finishing this one, it proves you're committed to your launch. You're the type of person who finishes what they started, which is a vital quality for anyone who's about to launch a product.

It's time to make a commitment to yourself and to your product launch. I don't want this to be another book that you read and get inspired by, but don't follow through on.

Remember, there is never going to be a "perfect time" to launch your product. You'll have to get started before you think you're ready, and there will be challenges along the way. Maybe you'll have to work some nights and weekends. Maybe you'll lose a little sleep. The path to bringing your product idea to life won't be easy. But it will be worth it.

Don't find yourself a year from now regretting that you didn't get started. The time to start is now.

Here's to your product idea being *Crowdfunded.*

Mark Pecota

P.S. If you found this book helpful, and especially if you've used the book to launch your product, please leave a review on Amazon and tell us your story!

LAUNCHBOOM PROGRAMS

At LaunchBoom, we do more than just launches. We have programs to help you through every stage of your journey to bring your product and business to life.

Want to learn more? Book a call with a LaunchBoom expert:

SCAN OR GO TO CROWDFUNDEDBOOK.COM/CALL

ONE-MINUTE ASK

Thanks for reading my book!

I'd love to hear from you – whether you have some feedback, or your own personal story to tell.

If you found my book useful, please take a minute now to leave a review on Amazon. I read every single comment and I find them very useful!

Your feedback helps me write better content in the future.

Scan the QR code or go to crowdfundedbook.com/review.

Thank you so much!

Mark Pecota

Made in the USA
Middletown, DE
10 October 2023

40515819R00210